THE DINOSAUR GOOD EATIN' PRAYER

Get Down on Your Knees

And Put Up Your Paws–

Thank the Good Lord

For the Use of Your Jaws

Dinosaur Bar-B-Que

Dinosaur Bar-B-Que:
An American Roadhouse

Over 100 Recipes from the
Dinosaur Bar-B-Que,
Syracuse, New York

**Text and Recipes
by John Stage and Nancy Radke**

**Photography
by James Scherzi**

**Jacket and Book Design
by Holly Boice Scherzi**

Ten Speed Press
Berkeley / Toronto

Ten Speed Press
PO Box 7123
Berkeley, California 94707
www.tenspeed.com

Distributed in Australia by Simon and Schuster Australia, in Canada by Ten Speed Press Canada,
in New Zealand by Southern Publishers Group, in South Africa by Real Books, and in the United
Kingdom and Europe by Airlift Book Company.

Jacket and book design by Holly Boice Scherzi
Photography copyright © 2001 by James Scherzi

Copy Editors: Margrit Diehl and Rebecca Pepper
Project Editors: Meghan Keeffe and Lorena Jones
Photography Assistants: Dan Guzelak, Joe Scherzi, and Jennifer Dargan
Food and prop styling: Nancy Radke with assistance from Martha Williams
Dinosaur Bar-B-Que liaison: Abigail Doyle
Mural painting on end papers © 1991 and on the table of contents page © 1989 by Jeff Davies
Paintings of James Cotton and Roland Kirk on page 128 © 1991 by George Frayne,
Commander Cody

The Dinosaur Bar-B-Que Restaurant Logo is a registered trademark of Dinosaur Bar & Char, Inc.

Library of Congress Cataloging-in-Publication Data
Stage, John, 1960–
    Dinosaur Bar-B-Que : an American roadhouse : over 100 recipes from the Dinosaur
Bar-B-Que, Syracuse, New York / text and recipes by John Stage and Nancy Radke ;
photography by James Scherzi.
        p. cm.
    Includes index.
    ISBN 1-58008-265-3 (hardcover)
    1. Barbecue cookery. 2. Dinosaur Bar-B-Que (Restaurant)
    I. Radke, Nancy, 1952– . II. Title.
TX840.B3 S722 2001
641.7'6—dc21   2001000391

First printing, 2001
Printed in China

7 8 9 10 -- 06 05 04

We dedicate this book to the staff
of the Dinosaur Bar-B-Que.

We'd also like to express our gratitude to all of our great customers who
continue to endure the lewdness, the crudeness, the noise, and the
general chaos of our happy little restaurant.

Acknowledgments

John Stage

I'd like to send out special thanks to all the Dino people who have helped make this book possible, especially the staff at both the Syracuse and Rochester restaurants and my partners, Mike Rotella, Larry Luckwaldt, and Nancy Luckwaldt.

For their shared commitment to excellence and service, thanks also go to our extended Dinosaur family of purveyors, who provide us with the finest quality ingredients.

And then there are our customers, our blues performers, and our friends; without them none of this would make any sense.

I'd also like to thank my mother and sisters for always having good food on the table, my father for keeping cold beer in the fridge, and my son, Dylan, for stretching his teenage palate.

The Garcia family in Miami helped to shape my culinary skills. They offered me hospitality and introduced me to the world of Cuban cooking. I'll always be grateful.

Finally, thanks to Nancy Radke, Jim Scherzi, and Holly Scherzi, as well as to the cookbook team of Martha Williams, Margrit Diehl, Rebecca Pepper, Dan Guzelak, Joe Scherzi, and Jennifer Dargan. It's been a pleasure and a tremendous learning experience working on this book with you.

Nancy Radke

I'd like to thank my family, who has always been there to eat every version of every recipe, especially my husband, Gary, whose wholehearted support means everything to me; my daughter, Lydia, who has the most discriminating taste buds in the world; and Bob and Sue Romig and Ruth and Ray Radke, the best parents and in-laws a girl could ever have.

Then there are the folks who opened up the world of barbecue to me. Special thanks to my co-author, John Stage, for teaching me how to smoke a mean pork butt and use seasonings with abandon and skill, as well as the staff of the Dinosaur Bar-B-Que, who were always available to answer my questions and show me the inner workings of the pits, kitchen, and restaurant.

Debbie Van Ausdale greatly helped my research for the book by giving me my first ride on a Harley, as well as some valuable insights into the joys of riding motorcycles.

My cooking buddy, Martha Williams, whose advice makes me crazy and keeps me honest, helped out in so many ways during the project, and my cleaning buddy, Nora Jacobs, helped me return my kitchen to its pristine state after wild recipe-testing sessions. I cannot thank you both enough.

The folks at Ten Speed Press were extremely supportive of our first venture into the world of publishing and deserve special commendation, especially Dennis Hayes, who put the book team together, Meghan Keeffe, who shepherded us through the editorial process, and Phil Wood, Kirsty Melville, Lorena Jones, and Nancy Austin, who patiently waited for us to produce the book.

Last but not least, I'd like to thank Margrit Diehl and Rebecca Pepper for their wonderful editorial work, and my colleagues Jim Scherzi and Holly Scherzi for putting the Dino vibe into the book.

Contents

BAR B QUE

PIG IN

PIG OUT

Introduction

The Dino Story: Bikers, Blues, and Barbecues

History has a funny way of writing itself—of taking on a life of its own. So when folks ask me how we came up with the idea to start a honky-tonk blues barbecue joint in Syracuse, New York and name it Dinosaur Bar-B-Que, all I can say is "evolution."

We hatched the idea for the Dinosaur Bar-B-Que in 1983 at the Harley Rendezvous, a massive motorcycle gathering near Albany, New York. They had plenty of everything there except good food. Hanging with my buddies, Dino and Mike, and being the hungry men we always were and the good cooks we fancied ourselves to be, we found the pickin's slim. A few cases of beer later, some rotgut grub in our bellies, and absolutely nothing to lose, we decided to get into the business of feeding bikers. Hell, we were at these gigs anyway, might as well make a few sheckles.

When we sobered up the next day, it still seemed like a good idea to us. We were good cooks, we loved to eat, and most importantly, we believed that bikers deserved a decent plate of food! All fired up, we decided we were going to hit all the biker gigs up and down the East Coast. Throwing in the swap meets, tattoo shows, and club functions, we were sure we had a recipe for success. So who cared if we never had any food service experience?

Armed with this battle plan, we needed a name. It did not take long to come up with Dinosaur Productions. After all, Dino was a partner and a big SOB to boot. That seemed to fit. Then there was a Hank Williams Jr. country song called "Dinosaur" about a guy who revisited his favorite honky-tonk only to find, much to his chagrin, that they had turned it into a disco. We could definitely relate. And it was the '80s and we were all riding some prehistoric bikes—mine was a '57 Panhead, Dino's was a '55 Flathead, and Mike's was a '67 Triumph. That did it. Calling our new venture Dinosaur Productions just made sense.

We thought we were on the right track. We had a name, we had a plan, but there was a hitch. We had about $1.98 between the three of us. No bank back then was going to invest in this motley crew, so we did what we had to. We improvised. Once we got done sawing a 55-gallon drum in half and borrowing some used restaurant equipment, we were in business. Our first gig was a local swap meet.

We had a simple three-sandwich menu. I manned the flattop and kept the coils of Italian sausage sizzling next to glistening heaps of sliced onions and fresh red and green peppers. Mike and Dino alternated on the charbroiler, where they flipped burgers and grilled Delmonico rib eye steaks (always hand cut). We were picky bastards even back then, making quality our first priority right from the start.

The first step in our business evolution came the next year when in 1984 we changed our name to Dinosaur Concessions. We were living the true gypsy life on the road, traveling from town to town and always looking for the next big gig. Our circuit expanded to include some non-biker functions like state fairs and regional festivals. They weren't as much fun as the biker bashes, but they kept us rolling along. Every show turned out to be a crapshoot. We'd score big on one and lose our ass on the next two. Like the time we ordered 2,000 pounds of chicken for a concert where 10,000 people were expected. Things didn't go as planned, and we were lucky if we sold fifty pounds. Needless to say, we ate a lot of freakin' chicken that winter. We even used chicken as currency to pay off our less-than-thrilled employees and creditors, who suffered through that fiasco with us.

Big changes came in 1985. Dino retired and moved to Arizona to take care of some family business. Meanwhile, Mike and I were working on a secret weapon—our own homemade BBQ sauce to slather on our popular sandwiches. We were so excited by this that it prompted another name change. Dinosaur Bar-B-Que said it all.

Time went on, and the road seemed to get longer and longer. We were still diggin' it: riding our bikes to places we'd never been, and getting off on the thrill of the unknown. We had some wild times—to say more would be unfit to print in a nice family cookbook like this. Things were good, but during our midnight rides, our conversations kept turning toward owning our own joint. Our fast and loose carney-life was getting more and more regulated. We started thinking that if we had to live by the rules, we'd rather deal with one set versus all the variables we found in every town, county, and state we happened to be serving food in.

By the time 1987 rolled around, we were getting pretty burned out. Life on the road was definitely feeling more like a grind than the adventure it once had been. For the first time in our lives settlin' down sounded appealing. We found the perfect place in the old N & H Tavern in downtown Syracuse, New York. The N & H was a legendary "shot and a beer joint" that served good home cooking and was located under the local motorcycle shop. It was beautiful.

We had to stay on the road, though, in order to fund the remodeling of the restaurant. So we hung in there, a much easier task now that we had our goal in sight. But as fate would have it, something happened that changed our course one more time. We were in Hagerstown, Maryland, when some old southern guy came up and asked us why we called ourselves a Bar-B-Que. Sure, he had enjoyed his Delmonico sandwich with our special BBQ sauce on it, but he said that it wasn't real barbecue. Real barbecue was about slow fires, open and closed pits, and hickory wood. The more this good ol' boy went on, the more intrigued I became.

It hit me that Mike and I were just two guys of Italian descent from Central New York. What the hell did we know about real southern barbecue? That was about to change.

Determined to unlock the mysteries of the kind of barbecue that old coot planted in my head, I got on my bike and headed south. Back then, the books on the subject were few and far between, so I figured first-hand experience would be my best teacher. I ate

myself silly with barbecue, starting in Virginia and then riding on down to North Carolina, Tennessee, and Mississippi. At each stop I'd ask the locals where to get the best barbecue in town. I remember being blown away by the taste of smoke-infused meat. Little by little I asked questions and worked hard to pick up the southern barbecue vibe. It was kind of like penetrating a secret society. My final destination was Memphis. For me it was the Shangri-la of barbecue. By the time I headed back north, I knew what had to be done. True blue barbecue had become my passion. We had to get into slow-smokin' meat in a hickory-wood-fired pit.

Success is an elusive thing. When we finally opened the doors to the Dinosaur Bar-B-Que in the fall of 1988, we were expecting the same slam-bang action of the road. But the reality of our new venture was just

the opposite. Being the action junkies we were, the slowness of the place took the wind out of our sails. No action, no paychecks—what the hell was going on? To say times were lean would be an understatement. It was a good thing we were in the restaurant business or we would've starved to death. Looking back, if we hadn't been so hardheaded, we would have closed our doors on a few occasions. But there always seemed to be a glimmer of hope, so we stuck it out.

By 1990 we started turning things around. After the 1,000th person asked for beer with their barbecue, something clicked, and we decided to take another chance by expanding the joint and adding a bar. Of course, this was easier said than done.

To fund this new caper, we brought on old friends Nancy and Larry Luckwaldt as partners and embarked on the next evolutionary phase of the Dinosaur Bar-B-Que. Opening the bar turned us from a grab-and-go joint to a full-service restaurant overnight. Suddenly we had to learn this whole full-service, full-bar thing in a hurry. Lucky for us, we were fast learners.

We found that the restaurant biz was a lot like a Broadway show. When the curtain goes up, you better be ready. Our saucy wait staff brings the show to the table. Giving great service, having fun, and mingling with our customers is their mission. If you want your chops busted, they'll bust 'em; if you want to be left alone, they'll respect your space. Every table gets their own unique Dinosaur experience played to their expectations. It's the down-to-earth real life vibe of the joint that our wait staff feeds on with the energy and focus of all good performers.

Speaking of performers, we always played the blues as background music at the restaurant. It's just what we like listening to, and it's a natural companion for our barbecue. I can't remember the exact circumstances behind the decision to get into live music, but one fall Thursday in 1992 we had Dr. Blue, a local blues guitar solo artist with a big booming voice, perform live. Suddenly Thursday night became Live Blues Night. Well, that just felt so good, the next thing you knew, we had live local, regional, and national blues six to seven nights a week.

From the walls of the stalls

—Dinosaur staff and patrons

Dinosaur patrons are among the finest bathroom graffiti writers in the world. Just give 'em a pen and they'll leave their mark. This is not your ordinary B.J. loves C.M. stuff. The walls are filled with philosophy, advice, sex tips, and plenty of humor.

How 'bout this fashion advice from the ladies' room: "You'd be surprised how much it costs to look this cheap." Or this cheap shot: "What's the difference between men and government bonds? Bonds mature!" Don't worry, the guys get in their licks as well with observations like this: "Love at first sight is just lust with potential." They also have some advice for the ladies: "If a woman can read the writing on the wall, she's in the wrong restroom."

Every once and a while the walls get so filled up that we have to paint 'em. This way the creativity of our diners can flow once again. We like their contributions so much that we've included some of their best material throughout the book. Just look for the little outhouse and enjoy the wit and wisdom—you'll laugh, you'll cry, you'll think.

There have been many great acts that have graced our stage over the years, from the old blues legends like Clarence Gatemouth Brown, Jimmy Rodgers, and James Cotton to our vast array of local blues talent. It was a personal thrill when we first booked the Nighthawks, an act out of D.C. Back in the mid '70s they pretty much turned me on to the blues, and so booking them was a real kick. Honestly, there's not enough room to list all the magical musical moments we've had at the Dinosaur, but it sure does make us feel fortunate to have been a part of the scene.

Lord knows, we've had our fun and we've made our mistakes, but the only constant throughout the years has been our unyielding dedication to serving the freshest, highest quality food we can. I guess that for a self-taught guy like me, learning about food is what drives me onward, and it's the reason why I love this crazy business.

Like I said, we've always been picky about quality. I think that comes from our Italian mothers and grandmothers, who taught us that the best food begins with the freshest and finest raw ingredients— never fancy, but always good. We strive to treat those ingredients with respect, working to achieve honest, direct flavor in our food. After all, with barbecue, we're dealing with just four essentials: meat, spice, smoke, and sauce. Great barbecue is all about fusing the perfect balance between those four things. No one element should predominate; they all should compliment each other in perfect harmony.

Our menu is firmly rooted in the traditions of southern barbecue. But there are other influences that shape our flavors and give our food its own distinctive character. That's one of the secrets of great barbecue—staying committed to tradition, but finding your own stamp and signature.

My life experiences have dramatically shaped our Dinosaur cooking style. I always enjoyed great Italian food as a kid. Then I learned about the incredible culinary traditions of Cuba during my stays in Miami, and got turned on to the bright flavors of Asia during a stint cooking at a sorority under the guidance of Mrs. M., an incredible Japanese chef. Road trips to Louisiana taught me all that was good about Cajun and Creole cooking. But the places I loved the most and that helped shape our Dinosaur daily menu were the good old homestyle "meat and three" restaurants found along the rural roads and in the small towns all over the South. Just like them, we serve up our grub with a selection of sides chosen from our long list of favorites.

But the flavors and cooking styles that I experienced over the years really come alive in our Custom-Que Menu, which enables me to stretch out a bit without disturbing our traditional menu. I'm happiest when I'm cooking, and our specials keep the creative juices flowing. Our Dinosaur Bar-B-Que Sensuous Slathering Sauce, which we refer to as "the Mutha Sauce" in this book, acts as a launching pad for the many flavor directions we like to explore in the specially sauced dishes we create. Nothing's too fancy, but everything's gotta have a good, distinctive, bold taste.

Our customers wouldn't want it any other way. All you have to do is look at our clientele, which includes people from all walks of life, and it shows you how barbecue is the great equalizer. It brings people together who wouldn't normally be socializing, satisfies their cravings, and makes them happy to be spending time in the same honky-tonk joint.

Looking back, it's been a wild ride. I wish I could say that every move we made was carefully studied, planned, and executed. In reality, if the idea seemed right, we just did it. The lessons came later. It's probably not the best way to build a business, but it has definitely been the Dinosaur way. Like the old saying goes, if you don't roll the dice, you'll never get a seven. We've been gambling for years, and as long as we continue to enjoy the business and have a couple of crazy ideas in our heads, the evolution of the Dinosaur Bar-B-Que is bound to continue.

Dinosaur Top Twenty-One

(Background music favorites played every day at our joint.)

1. Hank Williams Jr., "Whiskey Bent and Hell Bound"

2. Magic Sam, "West Side Soul"

3. Muddy Waters, "Trouble No More"

4. Albert King, "Let's Have a Natural Ball"

5. William Clark, "Groove Time"

6. David Allen Coe, "Greatest Hits"

7. Louis Jordon, "Best of Louis Jordon"

8. Waylon Jennings, "Lonesome, Ornery & Mean"

9. Jimmy Johnson, "Johnson Wacks"

10. Otis Rush, "Lost in the Blues"

11. Clarence Gatemouth Brown, "Standing My Ground"

12. Johnny Copeland, Albert Collins, Robert Cray, "Showdown"

13. Fenton Robinson, "Night Flight"

14. Charlie Musselwhite, "Ace of Harps"

15. The Nighthawks, "Ten Years Live"

16. Eddie Taylor, "I Feel So Bad"

17. Luther Tucker, "Sad Hours"

18. T-Bone Walker, "Cold, Cold Feeling"

19. The Rolling Stones, "Exile on Main Street"

20. Roy Buchanan, "When a Guitar Sings the Blues"

21. Little Walter, "Greatest Hits"

Mark Wenner and Pete Kanaris of the Nighthawks

Clockwise: Miss Honey of Rod Piazza and The Mighty Flyers; Phil and Mike Petroff; Sweet Curtis Brown

Clockwise: Colin Aberdeen; Scott Sterling, our sound guru; Mark Hoffmann and Mark French

Techniques of Outdoor Cookin'

Cooking over live coals is the oldest technique on the books. It dates back to the caveman. Even today, hanging with the "tribe" and slowly cooking a hunk of meat til it slides off the bone all juicy and succulent makes us feel at a primal level that this is real food at its sensuous best.

Barbecue is a part of the evolution of outdoor cooking. The beauty of it is that barbecue goes beyond just cooking and becomes a gradual flavor-melding process that combines spice, meat, smoke, and sauce in perfect balance. The other great thing about barbecue is that you can take a rough, tough piece of meat, like a slab of beef brisket or a pork butt, and through the magic of barbecue, completely transform it into meat as tender as a filet mignon. But it takes some technique to do it.

So just like it was for our ancient relatives, the main trick to cooking outdoors is learning how to build and maintain a fire. Recognizing that not everyone has a smoker, all our recipes direct you to cook with charcoal. We think it's the next best thing after wood for outdoor cooking. However, we realize that lots of folks have gas grills, so we've included some temperature guides so that you can do some recipe adapting to suit the reality of your own grill.

Here's what you're gonna need to get started cooking outdoors:

- Grill with a lid
- Chimney starter if you're working with charcoal
- Charcoal briquettes with as few chemical additives as possible or
- Hardwood charcoal
- Newspaper
- Matches
- Wood chips
- Aluminum foil
- Oven thermometer
- Instant-read thermometer
- Tongs
- Brush and a bowl for BBQ sauce
- Wire grill brush
- Patience and plenty of cold beer

Building and Maintaining a Fire Using Charcoal

First you open the grill up and pull out the grill rack. We like using a chimney starter rather than splashing the charcoal with lighter fluid, a method that can flavor your food with petrochemicals.

Pour the charcoal into the top of the chimney starter and then stuff one large sheet of newspaper into the bottom. With a match, light the newspaper in several places through the small holes in the bottom of the starter, and that pretty much does it. After about five minutes, hold your hand over the chimney starter to make sure that you feel heat. It will take 20 to 30 minutes for the coals to get hot. You'll know when the top coals look sort of half gray. At that point, dump the coals into the bottom of the grill and spread them all around.

Here's where you're going to have to get personally acquainted with your grill. Depending on its size, you might need a bit more or a bit less than one chimney to get the right temperature. In general, we like the two-chimney approach because that way you will always have hot coals at the ready to add to your fire when it cools down during a long-cooking recipe. It's also great when you have a lot of food to cook. You always want to add hot charcoal to the existing fire in your grill a few at a time, til you get the heat boosted to the right cooking temperature. It's never a good idea to add cold charcoal directly to the hot ones in your grill; it will take the temperature right down and could possibly put the fire out. Just one word of warning: you're gonna want to keep the chimney full of hot coals in a safe heat-resistant place where children, pets, friends, and family won't bump into it.

Smokin' with Wood

In the restaurant we smoke our meat with quarter-split logs of hickory wood, which doesn't work in the backyard grill. Instead we suggest using wood chips because they produce good results and are much more adaptable for gas or charcoal grills. We've found that by wrapping damp wood chips in foil and poking some holes in the packets, you can achieve a close approximation of the smoke penetration that we get in our pits. Often you'll notice that recipes in other books, or even on the packaging of the wood chips you buy, recommend scattering the chips on the fire dry. Ignore these recommendations. You'll just be wasting chips.

Instead, pour the chips into a bowl—about a cup and a half of chips will make one packet and you'll need 4 to 6 packets for the average true blue barbecue recipe. Cover them with water and soak them for 20 to 30 minutes. Drain and divide them between 4 to 6 12-inch squares of aluminum foil. Fold the foil around the chips and then poke some holes in the foil on one side so the smoke can escape. Once you've spread out the coals in the bottom of the grill, put the packets right down on the hot coals, hole side up. Replace the grill rack, place an oven thermometer on the rack, cover the grill, and let it preheat for about 5 minutes.

Cookin' Over Live Coals

After 5 minutes, check the oven thermometer to determine the temperature of the grill. Or you can take the temperature of the grill with an instant-read thermometer by dropping the tip down through one of the grill's vent holes. If the grill is hotter than the temperature recommended in the recipe, don't worry about it. Just be patient and let the coals burn down a little more, or put the meat in anyway and you'll find that in a half an hour or so, the temperature will be more or less where you want it. If it's still too hot, close the vent holes down, and if it's too cool, open the vents a bit or add a couple of hot coals. Resist the temptation to open the grill too often after the first temperature check. About once an hour will be fine for long-cooked foods.

Now it's up to you to just keep checking the food and working to maintain your fire at the right temperature for the recipe. After the cooking is done and you've eaten, try to give the grill rack a good cleaning with your wire brush. A warm grill always cleans up easier.

Styles of Outdoor Cookin'

We employ several styles of outdoor cooking in the book—from fast and furious grilling to low and slow true blue barbecue. Here's an explanation of each, from the hottest and fastest to the coolest and slowest.

Direct Grillin'

Direct Heat (high heat grillin') When we say, "crank your grill up high" or "lay a hot coal bed," we're planning on doing some hot and fast cooking. The internal temperature of the grill will be somewhere around 500°, but the actual cooking is done with the lid up on the grill. When you're grilling, you're looking to sear the outside of the meat, fish, or fowl and cook it quickly right over the heat source, just til it's cooked but still juicy. You've gotta be careful with this type of cooking because it's easy to overcook your food. Remember, you can always cook food more if it's underdone, but you can't give back juiciness to something that is overcooked. That's why it's a good idea to keep an instant-read thermometer close at hand and pull your food off the grill when it reaches the right degree of doneness (see Touch or Temp: How to Test Beef for Doneness, page 34, and Cookin' Perfect Pork, page 95).

Direct / Indirect Grillin'

Direct/Indirect Heat (medium heat combo technique) For this two-step cooking technique you're gonna have a hot side of the grill (direct) and a cool side of the grill (indirect). The heat source is on the direct side only, that's why we say, "mound up the coals on one side of the grill." Once the grill rack is put into position, the cooking usually starts out on the direct side with the lid up to sear the meat and caramelize it a bit. Then you slide the meat over to the indirect heat side and cover the grill to finish cooking. Usually this method is used for thicker cuts of meat that need a bit more gentle cooking to get done without getting charred. The internal temperature of the grill can be as low as 275° for fish to as high as 350° for roasts and thick cuts of meat.

Remember, these are relative temperatures. It can be a bit hotter or a bit cooler inside your grill, so you'll have to adjust your cooking times accordingly.

True Blue Bar-B-Que (low heat slow cookin') This is the classic technique for smoking meat, poultry, or fish. You set up the grill with a hot (direct) and a cool (indirect) side. A drip pan filled with about a half inch of water is set on the cool (indirect) side of the grill to catch the fat as it slowly oozes out of the meat and to keep the inside of the grill moist. Foil packets of water-soaked wood chips are set on top of the heat source on the hot (direct) side of the grill. Meat is never put over direct heat with this method. Once the grill rack is positioned, it's set above the drip pan on the cool (indirect) side of the grill right from the git go. The grill is covered and the heat should be 225° to 250°, which is the ideal temperature for the best smoke penetration and barbecue succulence. You folks using a gas grill can turn on one side of the grill and set the dial to 225° to 250° right from the start and hold it there. However, if you're using live coals, it's a good idea to keep a chimney of coals lit at all times to boost the temperature when needed. You always want to add hot coals to the fire. Cold ones will take too long to ignite and will drag your temperature right down. Remember, you'll need to replace the wood chip packets a couple of times during the first three hours of cooking as they get smoked out.

Dinosaur Bar-B-Que at the New York State Fair

Assumptions: Don't Let Them Ruin Your Barbecue

1) Never assume that just because you put all the pieces of meat on the grill at the same time, they will all be done at the same time. Every slab of ribs, every piece of chicken, every steak must be viewed as an individual. Some are gonna cook faster than others, some slower. Each one has its perfect moment of doneness, and you are the judge. Get familiar with your food—touch it, smell it, take its temperature if you have to—just let it reach its own personal moment of doneness.

2) Never assume that any cooking time in this book (or anybody else's, for that matter) is gospel. Remember, barbecue is more of an art than a science. Sometimes the wind can kick up and turn your grill into a blast furnace, or maybe it will start to drizzle or rain and cause the coals to die down. Often the fire that you laid has cool spots right where they should be hot. Stay creative and just keep workin' it. Art is a beautiful thing—especially when you can eat it.

3) Never assume that what the recipe is telling you to do totally matches your reality. I call it common-sense cooking. It's that ability we all have to judge when things aren't going according to plan and allows us to make adjustments or to completely start over. Blindly following a recipe is courting disaster. For instance, after I fry up meat in oil, I often like to add some onions and peppers to the remaining oil so I can scrape the bottom of the pan, incorporating all the tasty brown bits from the meat. But what if that oil got a bit hot and all the bits are burned by the time you take the meat out? Well, then you've gotta use your head and dump out the burned oil even if the recipe says to save it. Let your common sense prevail.

4) Never be afraid to make a substitution. Say a recipe calls for red onion and you only have yellow. Who cares? Use your yellow onion. Or maybe a salad recipe calls for asparagus but you like green beans better. There's no law that says you can't use green beans. A good recipe should inspire you to do your own thing; it's not the law, it's a guide.

5) Never assume that a recipe will make a dish taste the way you like. Raw ingredients change all the time. A late summer/early fall tomato will taste different than the one you buy in the winter. Even cans of tomatoes can vary. Just because you follow the recipe to the tee doesn't mean it will come out exactly right. That's why you've gotta taste it to know. Taste all along the way and especially taste at the end before serving. Then you can tweak those seasonings and adjust the recipe to your ingredient reality.

Monsieur

Get Personal with Your Pit

Just remember that every pit and every grill, whether it's fired with charcoal or gas, is an individual. The more familiar you get with it, the more you get to know its delights as well as its quirks and foibles. We've found that it's a whole lot easier to get acquainted with your cooking partner if you give your pit or grill a name.

When we named our mobile catering pits, we had a bomb theme going on, dubbing them Lil' Feller, Fat Boy, and The Missile. Our two stationary pits are fondly referred to as The Coffin and The Doghouse. Then along came our biggest pit, straight out of the heart of Texas. This one had a commanding presence and soon became known as Monsieur—out of pure respect.

Our last pit went on its first catering job nameless. On the way home it slipped out of its hitch on the highway and flipped over a couple of times, spewing wood and some barbecue leftovers all over the road. The pit got a bit banged up in the process, but nothing that an industrial-sized frame stretcher couldn't correct. Back in business, we named her—what else—The Runaway.

All the recipes in this book were tested on Nancy's very humble backyard kettle-style charcoal grills named Bella and Hugo. So if you haven't taken the time to give your barbecue buddy a name, go do it. That way, you'll always have someone to talk to when you're doing some slow smokin' or fast grillin' in your own backyard.

Starters

Arepas

I first came across these tasty Colombian fried corn cakes stuffed with oozin', stringy cheese at a Miami street festival. Back home, I messed around with the recipe and added whole corn kernels to the dough to make 'em more interesting. In the restaurant we serve arepas with a pile of pulled pork in the center for a real Memphis-meets-Miami dish. But if you don't have the pork on hand, they're just as good served with some Fire-Roasted Garlic Salsa.

The Arepas
2 cups masarepa (precooked instant
    cornmeal—see note)
2 cups water
¼ cup sugar
2 teaspoons kosher salt
3 tablespoons butter

1 ½ cups canned, frozen, or fresh
    corn kernels, cooked
8 ounces mozzarella cheese, sliced
2 to 4 tablespoons vegetable oil

The Accoutrement
Fire-Roasted Garlic Salsa (page 24)

Dump the cornmeal into a mixing bowl. Set aside. Combine the water, sugar, salt, and butter in a small saucepan and bring to a boil. Pour it into the cornmeal and mix well.

Chop the corn kernels just a bit, and then mix them into the dough. Let the dough rest for 15 minutes. Divide the dough into 12 equal portions and flatten each one out with your hands into a 4- to 5-inch disk. Lay the disks out on a piece of waxed or parchment paper. Slap the sliced mozzarella evenly on top of 6 of them, and cover each with one of the remaining disks to make a sandwich.

Heat 2 tablespoons of the oil in a cast-iron skillet set over medium heat. Slip a couple of arepas into the pan. Cook about 2 minutes, til golden brown. Flip and cook about 2 minutes on the other side. Flip back to the first side and cook 1 minute longer; then flip one last time and cook the second side til well browned around the edges. Let them sit a couple of minutes before cutting each one into 4 wedges. Finish cooking and cutting the remaining arepas in the same way, adding more oil to the pan if needed.

Grab a platter or individual plates, arrange the arepa wedges around a bowl of salsa, and dig in.

FEEDS 4 TO 6

Note: Masarepa is available in groceries that sell Hispanic foods.

Bar-B-Que Chicken Wings

Central and Western New York is "wing country," so you've gotta have some good wings on your menu. Most places fry their wings according to the original Buffalo recipe, but we smoke ours. You can make them hot or mild on your grill just by changing the rub and the sauce you slather on at the end. We serve them with the traditional fixin's—Blue Cheese Dressing and celery sticks.

The Chicken

24 chicken wing pieces
¼ cup olive oil

The Accoutrements

Blue Cheese Dressing (page 170)
Celery sticks

Mild Wings

¼ cup All-Purpose Red Rub (page 167)
2 cups Mutha Sauce (page 165)

Hot Wings

¼ cup Creole Seasoning (page 167)
2 cups Hot BBQ Sauce (page 165)

Wings require a two-phase cooking process. First you render out the fat and tenderize the meat on a medium-hot grill, 325° to 350°. Then you crisp and glaze them over hot coals. You might find it useful to light another chimney of briquettes (see Techniques of Outdoor Cookin', page 12) when you give the wings their first flip after 45 minutes, so you can add a few fresh coals to boost the heat at the end for an absolutely perfect finish.

Get cooking by rolling the wings, olive oil, and rub of your choice (All-Purpose Red Rub for mild wings and Creole Seasoning for hot wings) together in a large bowl.

Fire up your grill and mound up the coals on one side. Spread the wings out on the other side of the grill, away from the coals. Cover the grill and cook the wings for about 45 minutes. Open the grill, flip the wings over, and switch them around—move the ones closest to the heat source off to the side, and move the ones on the outside edge closer to the heat source. (Remember to start another chimney of charcoal now.) Cover again and cook about 45 minutes more, til the meat is tender.

Add some nice hot coals to the fire, and flip the wings over the direct heat of the coals. You should hear them sizzle a bit. Without waiting, brush the wings with some of the Mutha Sauce or Hot BBQ Sauce, flip them again, and let them cook for about 4 minutes so that the heat can caramelize the sauce. Brush the wings again with sauce and flip them over to cook another 4 minutes on that side. Slather the wings with sauce one last time to glaze them, and pull them off the grill as they get done.

Serve with Blue Cheese Dressing for dipping, celery sticks, and plenty of napkins. FEEDS 4

Drunken Spicy Shameless Shrimp
with Brazen Cocktail Sauce

These delectable shrimp boiled in beer and rolled in lots of spice and garlic are our most popular appetizer. Their "a-peel" has always been in the roll-up-your-sleeves sloppy nature of eating 'em. There's nothin' polite about 'em, and that's the way we like it.

The Shrimp

2 bottles or cans (12 ounces each) domestic beer

½ cup cider vinegar

2 cups water

2 tablespoons Old Bay seasoning

2 pounds large shrimp in the shell

2 tablespoons minced garlic

2 tablespoons Creole Seasoning (page 167)

The Sauce

2 cups Mutha Sauce (page 165)

1 cup prepared horseradish

2 tablespoons Worcestershire sauce

Juice of ¼ lime

Juice of ¼ lemon

2 teaspoons Tabasco sauce

Pour the beer, vinegar, and water into a high-sided pan. Add the Old Bay seasoning, cover, and blast the heat up high. When it boils rapidly, add the shrimp. Cover again and cook for 2 minutes, or til the shrimp turn pink and the flesh is just opaque. Drain the shrimp in a colander and cover with a layer of ice to chill them down just enough to stop the cooking.

Throw the shrimp into a bowl and toss with the garlic and Creole Seasoning. (They can be eaten warm or chilled.)

Whip all of the ingredients for the cocktail sauce together in a bowl, and serve with that mess of shrimp. FEEDS 6 TO 8

"Big Easy"-Style Bar-B-Que Shrimp

This is the Dinosaur take on a New Orleans classic dish. Serve with a hunk of crusty bread for moppin' up the tonsil-tingling sauce. Whether you eat it as an appetizer or serve it as a main course spooned over some Perfect Rice, you've got a winner on your hands.

The Shrimp
2 pounds large shrimp in the shell
1 cup dry white wine
1 cup clam juice
1 lemon, sliced in rounds
Kosher salt

The Sauce
½ cup butter
1 cup chopped onion
Kosher salt and black pepper

2 tablespoons minced garlic
1 cup Mutha Sauce (page 165)
2 sprigs rosemary (each 4 inches long)
2 tablespoons Worcestershire sauce
Tabasco sauce
2 tablespoons chopped fresh chives

The Accoutrement
Good crusty bread or some Perfect
    Rice (page 117)

Peel the shrimp, leaving their little tails on; devein and set aside. Pile the shells in a medium saucepan and add the wine, clam juice, lemon, and a pinch of salt. Cover and turn the heat up to high, bringing the mixture to a boil. Lower the heat and simmer for about 15 minutes. Strain; you should have about ¾ cup of the shrimp stock.

Sling 4 tablespoons of the butter into a skillet set over medium heat. Add the onions, salt, and pepper and cook til soft. Toss in the garlic and cook 1 minute more. Splash in the shrimp stock and add the Mutha Sauce, rosemary, Worcestershire, and pepper to taste. Bring everything to a boil and give the pot a stir. Dump in the peeled shrimp and perk it up with a couple of dashes of Tabasco. Bring back to a boil, lower the heat, cover, and simmer for 2 minutes, or til the shrimp just turn pink.

Cut the remaining 4 tablespoons of butter into 8 pieces and fold into the shrimp. Sprinkle with chopped chives. Taste and season with salt and lots of freshly ground black pepper.

Ladle the saucy shrimp into soup bowls and serve with a hunk of crusty bread, or spoon the shrimp over some Perfect Rice.

FEEDS 4 TO 6

Creole Deviled Eggs

Folks might laugh, but I could eat deviled eggs all day. My mother made them for me when I was a kid, and I've loved them ever since. When we serve our spiced-up version on a catering job or make them for a Custom-Que appetizer, everyone just goes nuts. To buy Zatarain's mustard, see the Resources section (page 175).

The Eggs
12 large eggs
6 tablespoons mayonnaise
2 tablespoons Creole mustard (preferably Zatarain's) or spicy brown mustard
2 scant tablespoons finely minced celery

Black pepper
½ teaspoon kosher salt

The Garnish
1 rounded tablespoon snipped fresh chives
Creole Seasoning (page 167)

Set the eggs in a pan just big enough to hold them in one layer. Cover with water and slide the pan over a high flame. Bring to a boil. Pull the pan off the heat. Cover and let sit for 12 minutes. Pour off the hot water and run cold water over the eggs to chill them. Peel and cut in half lengthwise.

Scoop out the yolks, saving the whites, and transfer to a bowl. Mash the yolks with a fork and add the mayonnaise, mustard, celery, pepper, and salt. Mash everything again and mound the yolk mixture back into the whites.

Garnish with chives and a sprinkling of Creole Seasoning. Serve on a platter and watch 'em disappear. FEEDS 6 TO 8

Never criticize a man until you've walked a mile in his shoes, because then you're a mile away, and you have his shoes!!! —Dinosaur patron

Fire-Roasted Garlic Salsa

Come into the Dinosaur any night after work and eat this salsa at the bar with freshly fried tortilla chips. Back home, make it with the best tomatoes you can get your hands on.

The Salsa

2 ½ pounds vine-ripened tomatoes
1 bulb Roasted Garlic (page 170)
Pinch plus 2 teaspoons kosher salt
5 tablespoons finely diced red onion
2 tablespoons minced seeded jalapeño pepper
2 tablespoons fresh lime juice

3 tablespoons minced fresh cilantro
1 tablespoon honey
Black pepper
Tabasco sauce

The Accoutrement

Tortilla chips

Fire up the grill, a gas burner, or even the broiler. Set the tomatoes directly over or under the heat source and cook, turning often, til the skins just blacken. Peel, cut out the stems, and then cut them in half around their equators. Take each half tomato in your fist and give it a squeeze over a bowl to get rid of the seeds and juice. Dice the flesh and put it in a clean bowl.

Squeeze the garlic cloves out of their skins, add a pinch of salt, and mash to a paste. Mix into the tomatoes along with the remaining 2 teaspoons salt and the onions, jalapeños, lime juice, cilantro, honey, pepper, and Tabasco. Purée half the salsa in the workbowl of a food processor. Stir the puréed and chunky salsas together.

Heap the salsa in a bowl and serve with tortilla chips. FEEDS 6 (MAKES 3 CUPS)

Note: When made ahead, the salsa can get watery. If this happens, drain through a fine sieve and serve.

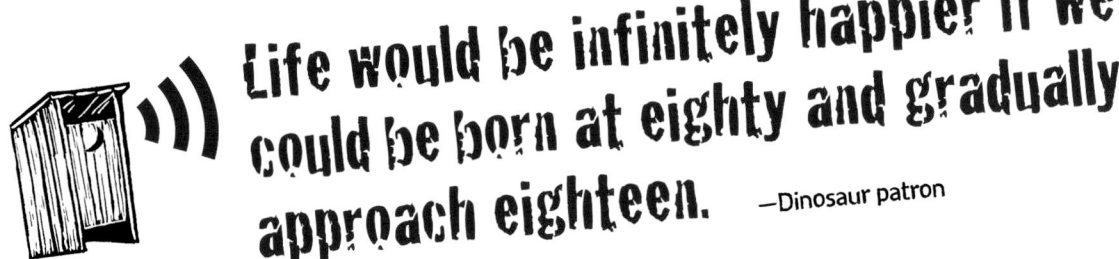

Life would be infinitely happier if we could be born at eighty and gradually approach eighteen. —Dinosaur patron

Grilled Scallop Ceviche

If you're looking for an appetizer with a summertime attitude, here's a simple, refreshin' recipe. The scallops grill up in minutes, and the tangy citrus marinade gets transformed into a delicious sauce.

1 ½ pounds sea scallops (preferably
    dry-packed)
2 tablespoons minced seeded jalapeño pepper

1 cup Mojito Marinade (page 164)
2 tablespoons finely diced red bell pepper
1 lime, cut into 8 wedges

Plop the scallops into a glass or stainless steel bowl. Combine the jalapeños and the Mojito Marinade and pour over the scallops. Marinate for 1 to 2 hours in the fridge.

Fire up the grill; then get back inside and fish the scallops out of the marinade. Dry them off really well, and string them onto skewers (see note). Pour the marinade into a small saucepan and bring it to a rapid boil. Toss in the red peppers, turn the heat to low, and simmer for 2 minutes. Keep warm.

Grill the scallops over the hot coals for about 2 minutes on each side, or til the edges are tinged with a rich brown color and the flesh turns opaque.

Ring a plate with lime wedges. Slide the scallops off the skewers and pile them up in the center of the plate. Pour on the sauce and serve family style, with a bunch of toothpicks so everyone can dig in.   FEEDS 4 TO 6

Note: If you're using bamboo skewers, soak them in water for 10 minutes before skewering the scallops; otherwise the wood will scorch on the grill.

Age is just a number, and mine is unlisted.
—Dinosaur patron

Guacamole with Fried Tostones

When we make guacamole, we make it to order. It's one of those dishes that doesn't improve with age. The avocados have to be perfectly ripe, giving gently when pressed, and then mixed with just the right balance of other ingredients. We serve our guacamole with warm, crisp tostones, a Cuban specialty made from fried plantains. You can make the tostones ahead of time and then refry them right before serving.

The Tostones
3 large plantains
3 cups vegetable oil
Kosher salt and black pepper

The Guacamole
6 tablespoons diced seeded tomato
2 tablespoons minced onion
1 tablespoon minced garlic

1 tablespoon minced seeded
    jalapeño pepper
3 tablespoons minced fresh cilantro
3 perfectly ripe avocados (preferably Hass
    from California)
1 ½ teaspoons kosher salt
Freshly ground black pepper
1 ½ tablespoons fresh lime juice
Tabasco sauce

Get the plantains ready for peeling by slicing the ends off. Cut each in half crosswise, and then make 4 long slits, just piercing the skin, down the length of each piece of plantain. Douse with warm water and soak for 10 minutes. Peel and cut on the diagonal into ½-inch-thick slices.

Heat the oil til hot but not smoking in a high-sided 12-inch skillet set over medium-high heat. Slide in the plantains and cook for 3 minutes, or til they're a light golden color. Take the pan off the heat. Fish out a few plantain slices at a time and sandwich them between 2 layers of parchment paper. Let them rest for a minute. Then, while they're still pretty hot, use a potholder to protect your hand while you press down on each parchment-encased plantain slice to smash it as thin as you can. (If you're making the tostones ahead of time, stop here. You'll be cooking them again in the same pan and oil to crisp and warm them right before serving.)

Start whipping up the guacamole by tossing the tomatoes, onions, garlic, jalapeños, and cilantro together in a bowl. (Cover and refrigerate at this point if you want to do this ahead of time.)

Cut the avocados in half lengthwise all the way around, and twist the halves apart. Pluck out the pit and then scoop out the flesh. Save the hollowed-out avocado shells to use as natural containers for the finished guacamole. Put the avocado flesh in a large bowl and mash with a fork, leaving it a bit chunky. Fold in the tomato mixture and give it a stir. Season it up with salt, pepper, lime juice, and Tabasco.

Right before serving, set the skillet with the oil back on the stove over medium-high heat. When the oil is hot, slip some of the smashed plantains back into the oil without crowding, and fry for about 3 minutes, flipping them over in the oil to get them crisp and golden brown. Drain on paper towels and season with salt and pepper while they're still warm. Continue frying the remaining plantains, adding more oil if necessary.

Mound the guacamole in a bowl or in the hollowed-out avocado shells, and ring it with warm tostones. FEEDS 3 OR 4

Fried Green Tomatoes
with Cayenne Buttermilk Ranch Dressing

Personally, I don't know why this is considered a southern dish. With our short growing season in Central New York, there's never a shortage of green tomatoes. It seems like the North should have thought of this dish first.

The Tomatoes

4 green tomatoes
Creole Seasoning (page 167)
2 eggs
Pinch plus 2 teaspoons black pepper
4 cups panko crumbs (Japanese-style dried
    bread crumbs—see note)
4 teaspoons kosher salt
½ teaspoon cayenne pepper
½ cup vegetable oil, plus more as needed

The Garnish

Grated Pecorino Romano cheese

The Accoutrement

Cayenne Buttermilk Ranch Dressing
    (page 171)

Core the tomatoes and cut off the ends. Slice them into ¼-inch rounds, and dry between several layers of paper towels to get rid of the excess moisture. Sprinkle lightly with Creole Seasoning on both sides.

Whisk together the eggs and a pinch of black pepper in a shallow bowl. In another shallow bowl or plate, combine the panko crumbs, salt, cayenne pepper, and the remaining 2 teaspoons black pepper. Dip the tomato slices in the egg mixture and then in the panko crumbs, pressing to coat them well on both sides and around the edges. Lift the coated pieces onto a rack set over a baking sheet. Pop them in the fridge for half an hour to set the crumbs.

Grab a heavy 12-inch skillet and heat the oil over medium heat. When the oil is hot, slide in a few tomatoes without crowding the pan. They should sizzle and bubble around the edges. Cook for 2 to 3 minutes on each side, til brown. Take them out of the pan, then add a bit more oil and get it hot before starting a second batch.

Drain the fried tomato slices on paper towels. Arrange them around the outside edge of a plate, sprinkle them with some grated Pecorino Romano cheese, and set a bowl of Cayenne Buttermilk Ranch Dressing in the middle for dipping. FEEDS 4 TO 6

Note: Panko crumbs are a bit coarser than other bread crumbs. They're definitely better for this dish. You'll find them in the Asian section of your supermarket or in Asian groceries.

Mississippi-Style Catfish Strips
with Spicy Tartar Sauce

We give catfish a good soaking in seasoned buttermilk before we coat and fry it.
It tenderizes and sweetens up the fish, which we serve with our favorite spicy tartar sauce.
You'll find it on our appetizer menu every day and in a sandwich on Fridays.

The Fish

1 pound catfish fillets
½ cup buttermilk
1 egg, slightly beaten
1 ½ teaspoons plus 2 tablespoons
  Creole Seasoning (page 167)
½ cup cornmeal
½ cup flour
3 cups vegetable oil

The Sauce

1 cup mayonnaise
¼ cup finely diced Garlic Dill Pickles
  (page 130)
2 tablespoons lemon juice
1 ½ teaspoons minced garlic
1 tablespoon Worcestershire sauce
1 teaspoon grated onion
½ teaspoon kosher salt
1 tablespoon minced fresh dill
1 ½ teaspoons lemon pepper
Tabasco sauce

Slice the catfish into strips ¾ inch wide by 5 to 6 inches long. Toss in a bowl along with the buttermilk, egg, and 1½ teaspoons of the Creole Seasoning. Cover and refrigerate for several hours.

Whip up the tartar sauce by stirring together the mayonnaise, pickles, lemon juice, garlic, Worcestershire, onions, salt, dill, lemon pepper, and Tabasco in a bowl. Cover and refrigerate til ready to use.

Set up your dredging and frying station. Line a cookie sheet with parchment paper. Fill a bowl with a mix of cornmeal, 2 tablespoons of Creole Seasoning, and flour. Pour the oil into a skillet. Slide the oil-filled skillet onto a front burner and get it heating over medium heat til hot but not smoking. Next to the stove, line up the cookie sheet, the cornmeal mixture, and the bowl of marinating catfish. Pluck the catfish from the marinade, drop it in the cornmeal mix, and roll it around in the mixture til coated. Then move the coated strips to the parchment-lined pan.

Once all the catfish strips are breaded, fry them in the hot oil in batches without crowding the pan. Cook, flipping once, for a total of 4 to 5 minutes, til nicely browned. Drain on paper towels. You might have to cook the fish in 2 or more batches; if you do, keep the fried fish warm in a 140° oven while you finish cooking. Have a plate ready, and, as soon as all the pieces are fried, serve with lots of tartar sauce. FEEDS 3 TO 4

Note: If you're making catfish to serve in a sandwich or as a fried fish dinner, you can keep the fillets large instead of cutting them into strips.

Pulled Pork Quesadillas

Because we're a barbecue joint, we've always got pulled pork on hand, so it was just natural for us to turn it into a delicious appetizer. Don't let our habits limit you. Make these quesadillas with some cooked turkey or chicken thigh meat or any chopped or shredded leftover meat you have lurkin' in the fridge.

The Quesadillas

3 tablespoons olive oil

¾ cup slivered onion

Pinch each of kosher salt and
  black pepper

½ pound Home-Style Pulled Bar-B-Que
  Pork (page 104) or slivered leftover
  cooked chicken or turkey thigh
  meat (about 2 cups)

¾ cup Mutha Sauce (page 165)

8 flour tortillas (6 inches in diameter)

1 cup shredded Cheddar or Monterey
  Jack cheese

½ cup well-drained Fire-Roasted Garlic
  Salsa (page 24)

The Garnish

Sour cream or Guacamole (page 27)

Pour 2 tablespoons of the oil into a skillet and set over medium heat. Add the onions, seasoning them with a pinch of salt and pepper. Cook til soft. Dump in the meat and give everything a good tossing. Add the Mutha Sauce and mix well. Set aside.

Film the bottom of a heavy skillet with a bit of the remaining olive oil, and set over medium heat. Put in a tortilla and cook on one side briefly, til tinged with brown. Take it out of the pan and continue with the rest of the tortillas, adding more oil if the pan looks dry. When they're all done, spread out 4 of the tortillas on a work surface, browned side up. On each one, layer ½ cup pulled pork, ¼ cup cheese, and 2 tablespoons salsa. Top each one with another tortilla, browned side down.

Film the skillet with oil again and slide in one of the quesadillas. Flatten with a spatula and cook til the bottom is crisp and tinged with brown. Flip and cook the other side. Remove to a cutting board and cut into wedges. Keep warm while you're cooking the rest. Serve with a dollop of sour cream or guacamole. FEEDS 4

Beauty is in the eye of the beerholder.
—Dinosaur patron

Sausage Bread

This is my version of a recipe that's been bouncing around my family for years. It's more Italian than barbecue, but who cares? It's definitely a crowd pleaser. We get our fresh bread dough from the Columbus Bakery, a legendary family-run bakery in Syracuse.

1 ¼ pounds Italian bread dough

2 tablespoons olive oil

1 ¼ cups chopped onion

1 cup chopped red bell pepper

Pinch each of kosher salt and black pepper

4 cloves garlic, minced

¾ to 1 pound bulk sweet Italian sausage

8 ounces sliced provolone cheese
   (about 10 slices)

¼ cup pitted, chopped kalamata olives

¾ cup grated Pecorino Romano cheese

10 fresh basil leaves

Remove the bread dough from the bag it was sold in, and shape it into a ball. Set it on a lightly oiled cookie sheet and cover with a dish towel. Let it rise at room temperature for about 1 hour, or til doubled in size.

Preheat the oven to 375°. Pour the oil into a large skillet. Fling in the onions and peppers, along with a pinch of salt and pepper. Sizzle over medium-high heat til soft. Toss in the garlic and cook for 1 minute more. Crumble in the sausage and cook, chopping and stirring to break up the meat into small pieces. Once it loses its pink color, slide the pan off the heat. Drain the cooked mixture in a colander and let it cool down.

Stretch the dough out into a 15-inch square. Cover with the provolone, leaving a 1-inch border around the edge. Top with the sausage mixture, followed by the olives and Pecorino Romano. Wash and dry the basil leaves, chop them, and sprinkle over the stuffing ingredients.

Grab the edge of the dough nearest you with two hands, and fold it up over the filling to the middle of the square. Flop the newly folded edge nearest you over again, this time three-fourths of the way up the square. Now reach over and bring the last part of the square—the part farthest from you—toward you and up onto the top. Pinch the dough together along the length of the seam and along the edges to seal.

Oil a large jelly roll pan, and carefully flip the loaf onto the pan, seam side down. Brush the bread with oil and bake for 45 minutes, til golden brown. Cool for at least 20 minutes, and then cut into 1-inch slices. Serve warm.

FEEDS 8 TO 12

Beef

Touch or Temp: How to Test Beef for Doneness

Perhaps the best way to test a steak on the grill is to give it a poke with your finger. By feeling the "give" of the meat, you can judge the degree of doneness without piercing it, which lets some of the juices run out. Here's how to practice this technique:

RARE Shake out your hand and touch your thumb and index finger lightly together. Poke the finger of your free hand into the fleshy part of your palm between your thumb and index finger. If the steak gives softly, like your flesh, it's gonna be rare inside.

MEDIUM-RARE Now touch your thumb and middle finger together. Feel how the muscle gets a bit more taut. That's what a medium-rare steak feels like.

MEDIUM Do the same thing with your thumb and ring finger. Now you've got the feel of a medium piece of beef.

MEDIUM-WELL TO WELL-DONE Personally I'd never cook a steak to this point, but if a guest or relative insists, touch your pinky and thumb together. Touch the same spot on your palm and it will feel very firm, like a well-done steak.

For those who like to use an INSTANT-READ THERMOMETER for precision, here are some temperature guidelines. Remember, cook steaks right to the temperature for the desired degree of doneness. However, pull a roast out of the oven 5° below the desired temperature. It will rise to the correct reading during the 15 minutes of resting time required after roasting.

RARE	120° to 130°
MEDIUM-RARE	130° to 135°
MEDIUM	140° to 150°
MEDIUM-WELL	155° to 165°
WELL-DONE	170° to 185°

Black & Blue Pan-Seared Beef Tenderloins

Pan Sear

Don't get me wrong from the title—I treat these tender babies right. First you blacken 'em in a smoking skillet and then finish 'em off with a blue cheese-studded BBQ sauce. If that's not respect, I don't know what is.

The Sauce

2 tablespoons butter

1 large shallot, minced

2 large cloves garlic, minced

3 tablespoons Worcestershire sauce

2 tablespoons freshly squeezed orange juice

1 teaspoon Dijon mustard

1 cup Mutha Sauce (page 165)

1 teaspoon kosher salt

3/4 teaspoon black pepper

2 to 3 tablespoons crumbled blue cheese

The Tenderloins

2 tablespoons kosher salt

2 tablespoons coarsely ground or cracked black pepper

4 beef tenderloin steaks (8 ounces each)

2 tablespoons olive oil

The Garnish

2 tablespoons sliced scallion

Fix up the sauce. Grab a small saucepan and sling it over medium heat. Toss in the butter and, once it's melted, add the shallots and garlic. Cook til they're soft. Throw in the Worcestershire sauce, orange juice, mustard, Mutha Sauce, salt, and pepper. Give the sauce a stir and keep it warm on a back burner. Crumble the blue cheese and set it aside in the fridge.

Fire up a skillet (cast iron works best) over high heat til smoking hot, about 8 minutes. While that's going on, mix up the salt and pepper on a plate and press the steaks into it, coating them on both sides. Swirl the olive oil into the pan and then throw in the steaks. Cook til they're a deep bronze color (not really black) on the outside and medium-rare on the inside. That'll take about 4 minutes on each side, but you can cook them longer if that's the way you like them (see Touch or Temp on page 34). Plate up the steaks and keep them warm in a 140° oven while you're finishing the sauce.

Throw the blue cheese into the warm sauce as quickly as you can, and give it a little stir. Pour the sauce over the steaks before the cheese melts completely. Toss a few scallions over each steak and you've got a real shiner. FEEDS 4

Direct Grillin'

Grilled Porterhouse
with Molasses-Bourbon Steak Sauce

Porterhouse is a great cut of beef. You get a piece of the rib eye, a piece of the tenderloin, and (my personal favorite) a piece of the fatty tail. Grilled and soused with Molasses-Bourbon Steak Sauce, it's a beautiful thing.

The Sauce

2 tablespoons butter
½ cup chopped red onion
½ cup diced red bell pepper
1 medium jalapeño pepper, seeded
   and minced
Pinch each of kosher salt and black pepper
3 large cloves garlic, minced
2 cups Mutha Sauce (page 165)

3 to 4 tablespoons Jim Beam or
   Jack Daniels bourbon
¼ cup molasses
3 tablespoons sliced scallion

The Steak

4 porterhouse steaks (18 to 22 ounces each)
Kosher salt and black pepper
Olive oil

Fix up some sauce. Turn the heat to medium-high and set a saucepan over it. Add the butter and, once it's melted, throw in the onions, peppers, and jalapeños. Cook til soft, seasoning it up with a pinch of salt and pepper. Toss in the garlic and cook 1 minute more. Swirl in the Mutha Sauce, bourbon, and molasses. Warm it up, then add half the scallions, saving the rest to sprinkle over the finished dish. Keep the sauce warm.

Fire up the grill. Rub the steaks down with salt, pepper, and olive oil. Grill over a hot fire to your liking (see page 34). Fling the steaks on a plate and give them a good sousing with the sauce. Sprinkle the remaining scallions over each portion before serving. FEEDS 4

Ten-Spice Strip Steak
with Soy-Ginger BBQ Sauce

Direct Grillin'

Back in the mid '80s I worked a semester as a cook for 38 college girls at a sorority at Syracuse University. A great gig if there ever was one. The Japanese housemother, Mrs. M., opened my mind to the freshness of ginger and other Asian flavors. You can find five-spice powder and hot chili sauce in the Asian section of your supermarket.

The Steak
1 ½ tablespoons five-spice powder
1 ½ tablespoons Creole Seasoning (page 167)
2 tablespoons soy sauce
2 tablespoons olive oil
4 strip steaks (10 to 12 ounces each)

The Sauce
1 tablespoon peanut oil
1 tablespoon chopped fresh ginger
1 tablespoon chopped garlic
Pinch each of kosher salt and black pepper
¾ cup Mutha Sauce (page 165)
¼ cup soy sauce
¼ cup water
1 teaspoon Sriracha Hot Chili Sauce (optional)
¼ teaspoon sesame oil
Juice of ⅛ lemon
½ cup sliced scallion

Mix up the five-spice powder, Creole Seasoning, and soy sauce in a bowl. Add the oil to make a paste and rub it over the steaks. For best results, do this in the morning.

Throw the sauce together when you get home. Set a saucepan on the stove and turn the heat to medium. Heat up the peanut oil and cook the ginger and garlic with a pinch of salt and pepper for 2 minutes. Add the remaining ingredients, saving 2 tablespoons of the scallions for garnish, and stir to blend. Keep warm.

Fire up the grill. Scrape off the seasoning paste where it's heavy on the steaks, leaving a light, even coating. Cook the steaks to the desired temperature (see page 34). Ladle the sauce over the steaks, and toss on those scallions you saved, to give the whole dish a little color. FEEDS 4

Churrasco Strip Steak
with Chimichurri Sauce

My first encounter with this dish was in a Nicaraguan steak house in Miami. The citrus-marinated steak with its beautiful green sauce just blew me away. Making the Chimichurri Sauce—a Latin version of pesto—takes no time, so you could easily fit this into your after-work grilling repertoire.

The Steak
4 strip steaks (10 to 12 ounces each)
1 cup Mojito Marinade (page 164)

The Sauce
1 medium bunch fresh Italian parsley
10 to 12 large cloves garlic, coarsely chopped

3 to 4 tablespoons freshly squeezed lemon juice (about 1 lemon)
1 teaspoon red pepper flakes
2 teaspoons kosher salt
1 teaspoon ground cumin
1 teaspoon dried oregano
1 cup extra virgin olive oil

Get up early in the morning and remove the bootstrap tendon sometimes found on the outside edge of the steaks, so they won't curl when you cook them. Pour on the marinade and let them soak up flavor all day.

Whip up a batch of sauce. Pick off the parsley leaves to make a packed cup. Toss them in a processor or blender with the garlic, lemon juice, red pepper flakes, salt, cumin, and oregano. Process to a paste, scraping down the workbowl several times. With the processor running, slowly dribble in the olive oil til fully blended. Taste and fix up the seasonings. Set aside.

Fire up the grill. Take the steaks out of the marinade and pat dry. Grill over hot coals til medium-rare (see page 34). When they're done, pull them off the grill and throw them on some plates. While they're still sizzling, spoon some sauce over each steak and let the flavors and aromas blow your mind. FEEDS 4

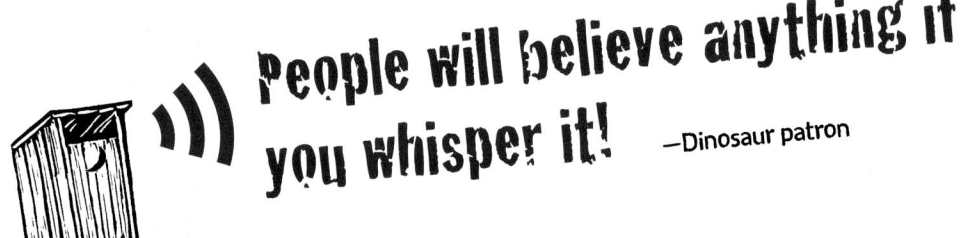

People will believe anything if you whisper it! —Dinosaur patron

Grilled Creole-Spiced London Broil
with Horseradish BBQ Sauce

I'm a big fan of horseradish. When it's stirred into BBQ sauce it takes beef to the next dimension. If you take a few minutes to start this dish in the morning before work, you'll be eating about an hour after getting home at night.

The Steak

- 1 London broil, flank steak, or top round (2 to 2 ½ pounds)
- ¼ cup olive oil
- 1 tablespoon Worcestershire sauce
- 2 tablespoons soy sauce
- 2 tablespoons Creole Seasoning (page 167)

The Sauce

- ¼ cup olive oil
- ½ cup chopped red bell pepper
- ½ cup chopped red onion
- Pinch of kosher salt
- Pinch plus 1 teaspoon black pepper
- 4 cloves garlic, chopped
- 1 ¼ cups Mutha Sauce (page 165)
- ¼ cup Worcestershire sauce
- 2 to 3 tablespoons prepared horseradish
- ½ teaspoon ground cumin
- ½ teaspoon molasses

Needle the London broil with a fork, stabbing it all over. Make a wet rub by mixing the oil, Worcestershire, soy sauce, and Creole Seasoning together. Give the steak a good rubdown. For best results, do this step in the morning for cooking at night, but you can get by with just 4 hours of marinating if you have to.

Make up a batch of sauce. Heat the oil in a saucepan. Fry up the peppers and onions til soft, seasoning them with a pinch of salt and pepper. Throw in the garlic and cook another minute to soften it up a bit. Blend in the remaining 1 teaspoon pepper, the Mutha Sauce, Worcestershire, horseradish, cumin, and molasses. Warm the sauce up just before serving.

Build a medium coal bed in the grill, or set the gas dial to medium. Dry off the steak and throw it on the grill. Turn it over every once in a while til it's a beautiful medium-rare (130° to 135°—see page 34), 20 to 25 minutes.

Slice the steak thin across the grain, saving all those tasty beef juices to stir into the warmed-up sauce. Spoon the sauce over the sliced meat and it's ready to serve.

FEEDS 6

Honky-Tonk Pot Roast

Oven Cookin'

If you want to make people stop, sit down, and eat, just put this classic comfort food on their plates. The rounds of corn on the cob give the dish a mellow sweetness.

The Roast

1 tablespoon plus a pinch of kosher salt

1 tablespoon plus a pinch of black pepper

¼ cup flour

1 boneless center-cut chuck roast
(about 3 ½ pounds)

¼ cup vegetable oil

2 cups chopped onion

2 cups chopped red bell pepper

1 cup chopped celery

4 bay leaves

1 ½ tablespoons minced garlic

3 cups beef broth or stock
(to make your own, see page 169)

1 cup Mutha Sauce (page 165)

4 ears corn on the cob, fresh or frozen

2 cups peeled and quartered sweet potatoes

2 cups peeled and quartered
all-purpose potatoes

1 teaspoon dried thyme

The Garnish

Sliced scallion greens

Preheat the oven to 325°. Mix together 1 tablespoon salt, 1 tablespoon pepper, and the flour and rub it thoroughly into the meat. Pour the oil into a big, heavy Dutch oven, and get it nice and hot over medium heat. Brown both sides of the roast til deep brown, 5 to 8 minutes per side. Take the meat out of the pot and set aside.

Dump the onions, peppers, celery, and bay leaves into the pot. Season with a pinch of salt and pepper and cook til soft and translucent. Throw in the garlic and cook for 1 minute more. Add the broth and the Mutha Sauce. Give it a good stir. Put the meat back in and bring the liquid to a boil. Cover with a lid and pop into the oven to simmer gently for 1 ½ hours.

Grab the corn on the cob and carefully slice each ear into 2-inch rounds. Toss the corn along with the sweet potatoes, all-purpose potatoes, and thyme in with the meat. Simmer for about 45 minutes longer, or til the veggies are soft and the meat is tender. Take the meat out of the pan and let it rest on a warm platter for about 15 minutes. Skim the fat off the surface of the pan gravy and if it seems a little thin, just reduce it on top of the stove. Fish out and toss the bay leaves. Slice the meat and cover with gravy and veggies. Sprinkle on the scallions for color before serving it up.

FEEDS 4 TO 6

Beef Short Ribs
Braised in BBQ Red Wine Sauce

Cook 'em low and slow. That's the secret to tender short ribs.
I like mine spicy, rich, and mahogany brown.

The Ribs

¼ cup flour

1 tablespoon Creole Seasoning (page 167)

8 beef short ribs (3 ½ to 4 pounds)

¼ cup olive oil

1 large onion, sliced into thin slivers

1 green pepper, sliced into thin slivers

2 jalapeño peppers, seeded and minced

3 bay leaves

Kosher salt and black pepper

4 large cloves garlic, minced

1 cup dry red wine

1 ¼ cups Mutha Sauce (page 165)

1 teaspoon dried thyme

¼ cup water

The Garnish

2 teaspoons chopped fresh Italian parsley

Preheat the oven to 325°. Mix up the flour and Creole Seasoning. Roll the ribs around in it til they're coated on all sides. Fire up a skillet over medium-high heat and add the oil. Brown the ribs til crusty on all sides, about 5 minutes per side. (If the ribs don't all fit in the pan at once without crowding, do them in batches.) Move the ribs to a baking pan just big enough to hold them close.

Pour off all but 2 tablespoons of the hot oil from the skillet. Toss in the onions, green peppers, jalapeños, and bay leaves and cook, scraping in all those tasty brown bits clinging to the bottom of the pan. Season with a big pinch of salt and a dash of pepper, and cook til soft and light brown; then add the garlic and cook a minute more.

Pour in the red wine and let it bubble for 1 minute while scraping the skillet again. Add the Mutha Sauce, thyme, and water and simmer for a couple of minutes til blended.

Douse the ribs with the sauce and cover the pan snugly with foil. Bake for 2 hours. Remove from the oven and uncover. Skim off the fat floating on the surface. Stir up the sauce and taste for seasonings. Give the ribs a flip, cover them up again, and pop them back in the oven for another half hour or so, til they're fork tender. Pull the ribs out of the oven, and fish out and discard the bay leaves. Reduce pan sauce if necessary. Serve each person 2 hot and steamy, well-sauced ribs sprinkled with parsley.

FEEDS 4

Texas Beef Brisket

In Tioga, Texas, Gene Autry's hometown, there's a place called Clark's where they make some of the best barbecue brisket on the planet. They say they smoke theirs for 3 days at 140°. But we're not gonna put you through all that. It just takes a dedicated pit boss with 6 to 8 hours to spare and a good technique to get the right smoke penetration and produce a juicy but well-done piece of meat in a fraction of the time. That sounds like a contradiction, but it's possible. All you need is an afternoon with plenty of beer on hand, a bit of patience, and the recipe that follows.

1 beef brisket (4 to 6 pounds)
2 tablespoons Creole Seasoning (page 167)
or All-Purpose Red Rub (page 167)

¼ cup olive oil
2 cups Mutha Sauce (page 165)

Check out the instructions in The Techniques of Outdoor Cookin' (page 12) and the Beef Brisket Pit Boss Tips (page 45).

Dump 6 cups of hickory wood chips into a bowl, cover with water, and soak for half an hour or so. Drain and divide the chips between 4 squares of aluminum foil. Wrap up into individual packets, poking holes in the top of each one. Set aside.

Pull off the grill rack and fire up the grill. While that's going on, needle the brisket all over on both sides with a fork. Mix together the Creole Seasoning or All-Purpose Red Rub and oil. Rub this all over the brisket. Once your coals are good and hot, pile them up on one side of the bottom of the grill, and set two of the wood chip packets right on the coals. Position a drip pan filled with ½ inch of water on the side opposite the coals. Put the grill rack back in place. Set the brisket, fat side up, over the drip pan, and close the lid. After about half an hour, check the grill temperature. It should settle down to around 225°. If it's hotter, close down the vent holes. If it's cooler, open them up a bit.

Check the temperature of the grill every hour for the next 6 to 7 hours and make adjustments. If the temperature dips down to 200° or less, add a couple of hot new briquettes to the pile of gray coals, close the lid, and open the vent holes a bit.

Reach into the grill with some tongs after the brisket's been smoking for 1 ½ hours, and remove the old packets of wood chips. Toss two new packets of foil-wrapped chips onto the coals.

After the brisket has been on the grill for 3 hours, you have achieved the necessary smoke penetration. Grab the meat with tongs, remove it from the grill, and wrap it tightly in foil. Return the foil-wrapped brisket to the grill and cover. Now you're sealing in the succulence of the meat as you continue to cook it to an internal temperature of 175° to 180°. This will take another 3 to 4 hours, so keep working to maintain an even grill temperature of 225° to 250°.

Give that finished brisket a rest off the heat in its foil packet for 15 minutes. Save all the roasting juices and skim off the fat. Slice the meat thinly across the grain. Fan the slices out on a platter and pour some of those roasting juices over them. Serve with some warmed Mutha Sauce to spoon over the meat at the table. FEEDS 8

Beef Brisket Pit Boss Tips

If for some reason you have trouble maintaining the temperature inside your grill or the weather should take a change for the worse, don't get bent out of shape. Once the smokin' is done, the brisket can be finished in a preheated 250° oven til it reaches an internal temperature of 175° to 180°. This will take about the same amount of time as on the grill.

If your brisket gets done before the rest of your meal, hold it, still wrapped in foil, in a 140° oven.

Check your smoke penetration. When you slice the meat, you'll see a rosy border all the way around. If that border is ⅛ inch, you're doin' a reasonable job of smokin' the meat. If it's ¼ inch, you're on your way to bein' a pit boss, and if it's ⅜ inch, come see me about a job!

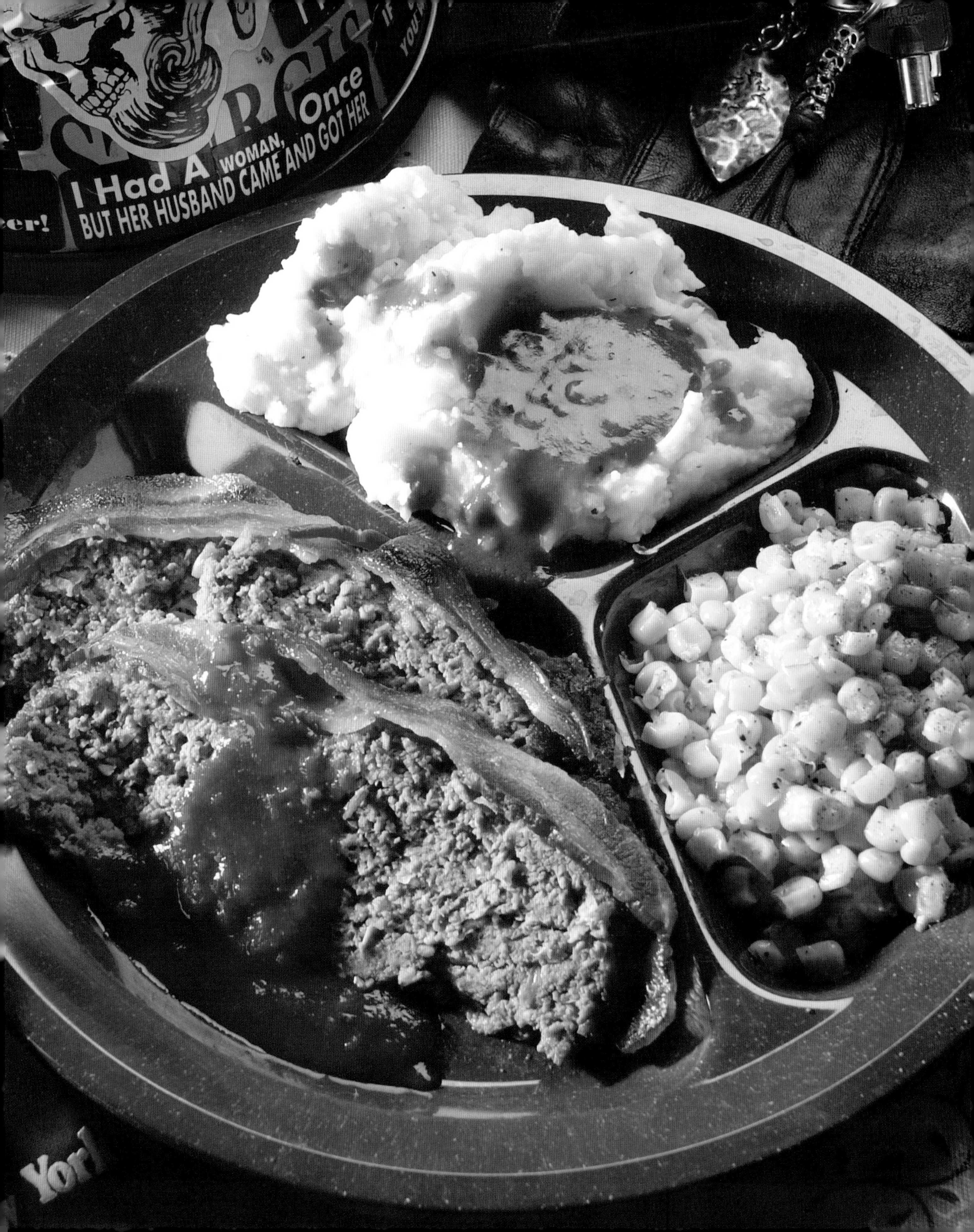
I Had A WOMAN, Once
BUT HER HUSBAND CAME AND GOT HER

Not Your Mama's Meatloaf

My mother is a great cook, but she never made meatloaf like this, and I bet yours never did either. It's the spice that gives ours its touch of creepin' heat. Way before meatloaf made a comeback on restaurant menus we were servin' it at the Dinosaur. It was our very first special.

2 tablespoons olive oil
1 ½ cups finely diced onion
1 cup finely diced green pepper
Pinch plus 1 tablespoon kosher salt
Pinch plus 2 teaspoons black pepper
1 heaping tablespoon minced garlic
1 ½ pounds ground beef

¾ pound bulk sweet Italian sausage
5 slices soft white bread
1 ¼ cups Mutha Sauce (page 165)
2 teaspoons chili powder
1 teaspoon ground cumin
⅛ teaspoon cayenne pepper
2 eggs, slightly beaten

Preheat your oven to 350°. Swirl the olive oil in a hot skillet. Toss in the onions and peppers with a pinch of salt and pepper and cook til soft. Add the garlic and cook just a bit more. Then scrape it all into a large bowl. Crumble in the ground beef and the sausage and mix everything together with your hands.

Take the bread over to the faucet and wet it down, then squeeze it out like a sponge. Chop it up nice and fine and throw it in with the other ingredients. Pour in ¾ cup of the Mutha Sauce and sprinkle on the chili powder, cumin, cayenne, 1 tablespoon salt, and 2 teaspoons pepper. Mix it all up with your hands. Add the eggs, and mix one more time.

Press the mixture into a 9 ½ by 5 ½-inch loaf pan. Slather on the remaining ½ cup Mutha Sauce. Pop it into the oven and bake for 1 ½ hours. Take it out and let it set 20 minutes. Pour off the fat. Slice into thick, comforting slabs. Serve with more Mutha Sauce at the table, so folks can ladle it on if they feel like it. FEEDS 6 TO 8

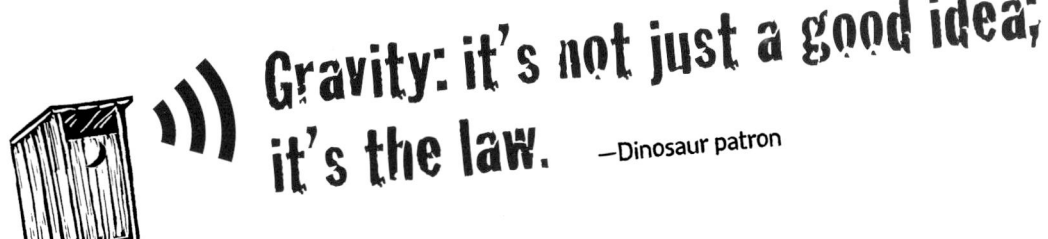

))) Gravity: it's not just a good idea, it's the law. —Dinosaur patron

Dinosaur-Style
Macaroni & Cheese
Shepherd's Pie

Here's a twist on a classic British pub recipe. The beefy base of the pie gets flavored up Dino-style and topped off with savory mac 'n' cheese instead of the traditional mashed potatoes. It makes a hearty meal. Just add salad.

3 tablespoons kosher salt
1 pound small pasta shells
2 tablespoons vegetable oil
2 cups chopped onion
1 cup chopped green pepper
5 large cloves garlic, chopped
1 ¼ pounds lean ground beef
1 tablespoon black pepper
¾ cup Mutha Sauce (page 165)

¼ cup butter
¼ cup flour
2 ½ cups half-and-half or milk
3 cups shredded sharp Cheddar cheese
1 cup freshly grated
    Parmigiano-Reggiano cheese
2 teaspoons Dijon mustard
Tabasco sauce

Preheat the oven to 375°. Bring a big pot of water to a bubbling boil. Add 2 tablespoons of the salt, and stir in the pasta shells. Cook til al dente. Drain, rinse in cold water, and set aside.

Throw a skillet on medium heat and swirl in the vegetable oil. Add half the onions and half the peppers, cooking them til soft. Toss in the garlic and cook for about 1 minute more. Dump in the ground beef, breaking it up with a spoon, and cook it with the veggies til it loses its pinkness. Season with 1 ½ teaspoons each of salt and pepper. Mix in the Mutha Sauce and take the pan off the heat.

Melt the butter in a large saucepan over medium heat, and fry up the rest of the onions and peppers til soft. Add the flour and whisk like crazy til very well blended. Slowly dribble in the half-and-half or milk, whisking as you go. When the mixture bubbles and thickens slightly, remove it from the heat. Stir in 2 cups of the Cheddar, the Parmigiano-Reggiano, mustard, and the remaining 1 ½ teaspoons each of salt and pepper. Spice the sauce up with Tabasco to your liking. Stir til the cheeses are melted, then fold the cheese sauce into the drained pasta and set aside.

Grease up a 9 by 13-inch baking pan. Spread the ground beef mixture in the pan, and then spread the mac 'n' cheese over it. Top everything with the last cup of Cheddar, and pop it into the preheated oven to bake for 30 to 45 minutes, or til the cheese sauce bubbles around the edges. Let the dish rest for 15 minutes before serving—if people can wait that long to eat it. FEEDS 6 TO 8

Garlic-Spiked Roast Beef
with Portabella Mushroom Sauce

Dino, our ever-vigilant head of security, is also a helluva good cook, though he hasn't ingested a vegetable since the mid '60s. This is how he makes roast beef, and this is how I like to sauce it—sneaking in lots of luscious mushrooms. Try to get your hands on the baby bellas. They're packed with flavor and slice up nicely into bite-size pieces.

The Roast

1 beef roast—sirloin, eye, round, or chuck
    (3 to 3 ½ pounds)
5 cloves garlic, each cut lengthwise in 3 slices
2 tablespoons olive oil
1 tablespoon Creole Seasoning (page 167)

The Sauce

12 ounces portabella mushrooms
¼ cup olive oil
1 cup chopped onion
¼ cup chopped red bell pepper
Kosher salt and black pepper
3 bay leaves
4 or 5 large cloves garlic, minced
½ cup dry red wine
1 ½ cups beef broth or stock (to make your
    own, see page 169)
2 tablespoons chopped fresh Italian parsley
Pinch of dried oregano
2 tablespoons heavy cream

Preheat the oven to 350°. Stab the meat with a thin knife and stuff the garlic slices into the slits. Make a loose rub with the olive oil and Creole Seasoning; then massage it into the roast. Let the roast sit in the rub for a couple of hours, if you've got the time, or cook it up right away.

Set the roast, fat side up, on a rack in a roasting pan. Roast for 1 to 1 ¼ hours, or til a meat thermometer hits 135° (see page 34).

Get to work on the sauce while the meat's roasting. Clean and chop two-thirds of the mushrooms, and slice the remaining third. Set aside. In hot olive oil, flash-cook the onions and peppers with a pinch of salt and pepper for about a minute. Add the chopped mushrooms and cook til nice and soft. Toss in the bay leaves and garlic and cook for 1 minute more. Pour in the wine and simmer for 2 minutes. Add the broth and simmer for 10 minutes more. Then add the sliced portabellas, parsley, and oregano. Give it a good seasoning with salt and pepper. Pull out and discard the bay leaves. At the very end, finish the sauce with the heavy cream. Keep it warm, but don't let it boil.

Slice the meat across the grain. Pour any juices that have collected on the cutting board or in the roasting pan into the sauce. Serve up the sliced meat with some sauce ladled over it. FEEDS 6 TO 8

Ropa Vieja
(Shredded Beef in Cuban Creole Sauce)

This Cuban Creole dish, whose name means "old clothes," knocks me out every time I eat it. You can cook and shred up the flank steak way in advance, then dinner is only half an hour away when you're hungry for some good robust Latin flavors.

The Steak

1 flank steak (1 ½ to 2 pounds)

Kosher salt and black pepper

2 tablespoons olive oil

1 carrot, cut in large hunks

1 medium onion, peeled and quartered

4 large cloves garlic, crushed

2 or 3 bay leaves

2 cups beef broth or stock (to make your own, see page 169)

The Sauce

¼ cup olive oil

1 medium onion, chopped

1 large green pepper, finely diced

1 or 2 jalapeño peppers, seeded and minced

Pinch plus 2 teaspoons kosher salt

Pinch plus 1 teaspoon black pepper

4 large cloves garlic, finely chopped

2 cans (16 ounces each) tomato sauce or 4 cups Mutha Sauce (page 165)

1 teaspoon ground cumin

2 teaspoons dried oregano

The Accoutrements

4 to 6 cups Perfect Rice (page 117)

10 ounces fresh or frozen sweet peas, cooked

2 red peppers, roasted, peeled, seeded, and cut into strips

Preheat the oven to 325°. Season the flank steak with salt and pepper. Schlepp a heavy 12-inch skillet over to the stove and heat the olive oil in it. Brown one side of the steak for about 4 minutes over high heat. Flip it over and add the carrots, onions, garlic, and bay leaves around the edges. Season everything with another pinch of salt and pepper. Brown the meat and veggies for 4 to 5 minutes more to get some nice caramelization going on. Add the broth. Bring just to a boil, cover, and pop into the oven and simmer til the beef is fork tender, 1 ½ to 2 hours.

Take the beef out of the pan and wrap it tightly in foil, saving all those tasty veggies and cooking juices. Let the beef rest for about 20 minutes, and then shred it with your fingers into long stringy pieces along the grain of the meat. Meanwhile, strain out the bay leaves and the veggies. Return the cooking liquid to the pan and boil everything down til you've got 1 cup of liquid. Mix the shredded beef back into the liquid in the pan.

Make a batch of sauce. Heat the oil in a skillet and cook the onions, green peppers, and jalapeños with a pinch of salt and pepper til soft. Add the garlic and cook 1 minute more. Stir in the tomato sauce. Simmer for 15 minutes. Season with the cumin, oregano, 2 teaspoons salt, and 1 teaspoon pepper. Add the shredded beef, simmer til heated through, and then check for seasonings.

Spoon Perfect Rice around the edges of a serving platter, and heap up the Ropa Vieja in the middle. Top it off with peas and red pepper strips. Let the feast begin.
FEEDS 4 TO 6

Note: The beef can be cooked and shredded a day ahead, if you've got the time.

Vaca Frita
Pan-Fried Shredded Beef Patties

Vaca Frita, "fried cow," is a citrus-flavored variation of the Cuban dish Ropa Vieja, "old clothes." These incredibly tasty, crispy fritters of shredded beef are so good, they'll give you cravings that you never had before.

The Patties

Ropa Vieja (page 52), made without the Cuban Creole Sauce
1 cup Mojito Marinade (page 164)
Olive oil for frying

The Accoutrement

Black Beans & Rice (page 120)

Pour the Mojito Marinade into the Ropa Vieja in the pan with the braising liquid, and mix it all up. Let the meat soak up all those good flavors for at least 4 hours.

Grab one handful of shredded meat at a time, squeeze out as much of the marinade as you can, and shape the meat into a flattened patty about the size of your palm. Cover the bottom of a large skillet with ⅛ to ¼ inch of oil, and get it heated up over medium. Add the patties and fry a few at a time in the oil, cooking them til crispy and richly browned on each side. Watch them carefully so they don't burn.

Slide the fried patties onto a plate and serve 'em up with Black Beans & Rice. FEEDS 6 TO 8

Chicken

Chicken Pit Boss Tips

Two things have always puzzled me. Why do some folks parboil chicken before putting it on the grill? And why do others slather on the BBQ sauce right from the start? Both can make for some pretty disappointing barbecued chicken.

When you parboil, you're just throwing away all the good chicken flavor. With the lid down on the grill, you can get the chicken cooked through to tasty perfection in just 45 minutes. And you should never slather on the sauce too soon. That's a recipe for chicken that's raw in the middle and charred on the outside. Instead, just rub the chicken with a spicy mix that will flavor the meat as it cooks. Then all you have to do is glaze the chicken with the sauce at the very end.

The secrets to really great chicken barbecue are simple. All you've gotta do is:

- Rub the chicken with a spice mixture the morning before cooking for deep flavor penetration.

- Cook it over a medium fire (325° to 350° for charcoal and 325° for gas), so there's a minimum of flare-up as the fat renders out.

- Position the grill rack as high above the heat source as possible to minimize charring before the chicken is cooked through.

- Cook with the lid down on the grill so you get some good convection heat circulating inside.

- Glaze the chicken with BBQ sauce for only the last 15 minutes of cooking. You don't want the sugars in the sauce to burn.

- Check the internal temperature of the chicken with an instant-read thermometer. When it reads 160° to 165°, it's done.

- Serve with lots of napkins, 'cause you're gonna want to eat it with your hands.

Charcoal Bar-B-Que Chicken

Direct Grillin'

Because we smoke most everything at the Dinosaur, when I get home I really enjoy the flavor that cooking over plain old charcoal brings out. It's that delicate chicken flavor touched with spice and caramelized barbecue sweetness that I'm after. It's easy to achieve, but you've got to follow some simple rules, so take a look at the Chicken Pit Boss Tips before getting started.

8 chicken quarters (leg and thigh, breast and wing, or a combination of both)
⅔ cup olive oil

7 tablespoons All-Purpose Red Rub (page 167)
2 cups Mutha Sauce (page 165)

Prep the chicken by breaking the joint between the leg and thigh, and trim away any backbone attached to the thigh. Tuck the wing tip under the spot where the wing joins the breast. Mix up the oil and All-Purpose Red Rub, and massage it into the chicken pieces. On the breast pieces you can even lift up the skin and massage the rub right into the flesh. Cover and refrigerate the chicken til you're ready to grill it.

Build a medium coal bed in your grill. It should register 325° to 350° with the lid down. Open the lid and position the rack as high above the coals as possible. (This keeps the skin from getting too charred before the chicken is cooked through.) Arrange the chicken pieces, skin side up, directly over the coals. Close the lid and cook for 25 to 30 minutes; then give the chicken a flip, skin side down, and cook, covered, for 20 minutes more, or til it has an internal temperature of 160° to 165°. Check the chicken, and push the pieces that look the most cooked to the cooler edge of the grill. Keep cooking the thicker pieces, moving them to the hotter spots on the grill til they reach the same amount of doneness.

Flip all the pieces skin side up and slather on the Mutha Sauce. Close the lid of the grill and cook for 10 to 15 minutes more to glaze the chicken. Serve with more Mutha Sauce for ladling. FEEDS 4 TO 6

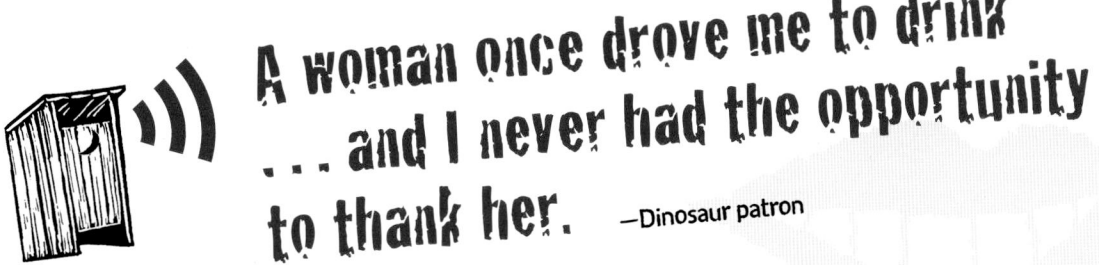

A woman once drove me to drink ... and I never had the opportunity to thank her. —Dinosaur patron

Bar-B-Que Turkey Breast

Direct / Indirect Grillin'

There are a couple of secrets to producing a juicy charcoal barbecue turkey. The first is to use a great bird. We use locally produced Plainville Farms fresh turkey, which is raised without the routine use of antibiotics (see Resources, page 175). The other secret is to get the spice rub up under the skin and then cook the bird over indirect heat.

1 turkey breast (3 ½ to 5 pounds)
¼ cup olive oil

2 tablespoons Creole Seasoning (page 167)
1 cup Mutha Sauce (page 165)

Flip the breast, skin side down, onto a cutting board. Take a chef's knife and carefully cut just through the breastbone, not the meat. Flip the breast again and flatten it out, using the heel of your hand. Mix up the olive oil and Creole Seasoning and smear the breast with it on all sides and even up under the skin. If you can, do this in the morning for evening grilling.

Fire up the grill, putting all the charcoal to one side. Put the breast, skin side down, directly over the hot coals for 5 minutes to caramelize the skin. Flip the breast over again, rib side down, this time moving it away from the coals to cook it over indirect heat. Cover the grill and cook for about 1 hour and 15 minutes.

Test the internal temperature of the meat by inserting an instant-read thermometer into the thickest part of the breast. When it reads 155°, slather the skin side of the breast with the Mutha Sauce. Close the lid and keep cooking to glaze the breast til the thermometer reads 165°, 15 to 20 minutes more.

Pull the breast off the grill and let it rest for 10 minutes before carving. Serve the slices hot with some more Mutha Sauce. The leftovers make great sandwiches.

FEEDS 6 TO 8

Grilled Chicken
with Chile-Pecan BBQ Sauce

Direct Grillin'

The bite of chiles combined with the sweet crunchiness of toasted
pecans give this saucy chicken dish lots of flavor and textural dimension.
In other words, you're gonna love it!

The Chicken

4 chicken halves or 8 chicken quarters
Olive oil
Kosher salt and cracked black pepper
Dried thyme

The Sauce

1 cup pecans
2 tablespoons olive oil
½ cup minced onion
4 to 5 large cloves garlic, minced

1 tablespoon minced, seeded jalapeño pepper
Pinch each of kosher salt
    and black pepper
1 cup chicken broth or stock (to make
    your own, see page 168)
1 ½ cups Mutha Sauce (page 165)
1 teaspoon ground ancho chile
½ teaspoon ground cumin
1 ½ tablespoons honey
2 tablespoons butter, cut in 6 pieces
2 tablespoons sliced scallion

Oil the chicken and season on both sides with salt, cracked pepper, and a sprinkling of thyme.

Build a medium coal bed in your grill. It should register from 325° to 350° with the lid down. Open the grill and arrange the chicken skin side up with the thickest parts to the center. Close the lid and cook for 25 to 30 minutes. Give the chicken a flip so the skin side's down and cook, covered, til golden, about 20 minutes more, or til it reaches an internal temperature of 160° to 165°.

Fix up a batch of sauce while the chicken's cooking. Toast the pecans in a 350° oven til fragrant and lightly browned, about 10 minutes. Chop them coarsely. Set aside.

Heat the oil gently in a saucepan over medium heat, add the onions, garlic, and jalapeños with a pinch of salt and pepper, and cook til soft. Pour in the chicken broth and the Mutha Sauce; simmer til reduced by a quarter, about 15 minutes. Add the chile, cumin, honey, and pecans. Keep warm. Just before serving, take the sauce off the heat and swirl in the butter, one piece at a time, til melted. Stir in the scallions.

Pull the chicken pieces off the grill and serve them smothered in sauce. FEEDS 4

Stuffed Chicken Highbrow

Direct Grillin'

As far as Dinosaur patrons are concerned, anything with goat cheese is kinda suspicious. Add some asparagus and you're tippin' the highbrow scale—hence the name of this dish. Many have discovered the tangy difference goat cheese makes when matched up with our Mutha Sauce.

20 thin asparagus spears
Kosher salt
2 cloves garlic, cut in half lengthwise
2 mild Italian sausages
4 whole boneless, skinless chicken
    breasts (8 to 10 ounces each)
Black pepper

5 ounces goat cheese
¼ cup sliced scallion
Olive oil
Creole Seasoning (page 167)
1 ½ cups Mutha Sauce
    (page 165), heated

Wash the asparagus and snap off the tough bottoms of the spears. Pour an inch of water into a skillet. Season with salt and add the garlic cloves. Bring to a simmer. Slide in the asparagus and cook til tender. Remove from the water, discarding the garlic. Set aside. In another skillet, cook the sausages whole and set aside.

Pull off the tenders from the inside of the breasts and save them for another use. Leave the breasts whole, and with the smooth side down, open like a book on a work surface. Flatten them with a meat/poultry pounder or mallet to ¼-inch thickness. Season breasts with salt and pepper. Slice the sausages thinly on the diagonal and place the slices on one side of each whole breast, leaving a thin border uncovered around the edge. On top of the sausage, layer 5 of asparagus spears, letting the points hang out at the ends. Cut 12 thin slices from the goat cheese, and put 3 on top of the asparagus on each chicken breast. Sprinkle with scallions.

Fold the uncovered lobe of each breast over the stuffed one to make a packet. Press around the edge to seal. Gently oil the chicken and season with salt and a light dusting of Creole Seasoning.

Build a medium bed of coals in your grill. Cook for 8 to 10 minutes on each side. Check the temperature by inserting an instant-read thermometer horizontally into the thickest part of one side, close to the stuffing. It should register 160°.

When the chicken breasts are done, take them off the grill, plate them, and serve with a little heated Mutha Sauce ladled over each portion. FEEDS 4

Note: If only thick asparagus spears are available, buy 10, cook them, and then cut each spear in half lengthwise.

Chicken Exotica

Indian spices and tandoori cooking inspired this one. The spicy, yogurt-based marinade tenderizes skinless chicken breasts to perfection. They cook up so tender you won't even need a knife.

The Marinade

2 cups plain yogurt

1 tablespoon grated fresh ginger

1 tablespoon minced garlic

⅓ cup fresh lime juice

2 tablespoons paprika

2 tablespoons kosher salt

1 ½ teaspoons ground cinnamon

1 teaspoon ground cumin

1 teaspoon ground coriander

1 teaspoon black pepper

1 teaspoon ground allspice

1 teaspoon mustard seeds

1 teaspoon honey

The Chicken

4 whole boneless, skinless chicken breasts
   (8 to 10 ounces each)

The Topping

¼ cup olive oil

1 medium onion, cut lengthwise into
   ¼-inch-wide strips

1 red bell pepper, cut lengthwise into
   ¼-inch-wide strips

Pinch each of kosher salt and
   black pepper

1 cup Mutha Sauce (page 165)

2 tablespoons chopped fresh cilantro

Mix together, in order, the yogurt, ginger, garlic, lime juice, paprika, salt, cinnamon, cumin, coriander, pepper, allspice, mustard seeds, and honey. Set aside. Make slits 3 to 4 ½ inches long on the top side of each chicken breast. Spread the breasts out in a shallow nonreactive pan. Cover with the marinade, and marinate at least overnight—they just get better and better the longer you soak them—even up to 48 hours.

Make the topping. Swirl the olive oil into a skillet and heat over medium-high. Toss in the onion and pepper strips and cook til soft, seasoning them with a pinch of salt and pepper; then add ½ cup of the Mutha Sauce. Cook a little longer, til thickened. Set aside.

Build a medium coal bed in your grill. Position the breasts—top side down first—and grill for 5 to 6 minutes. Then flip them over and cook them for another 5 to 6 minutes, or til done. Brush with the remaining Mutha Sauce right before taking them off the grill. This gives them a nice rosy finish.

Mound a spoonful of the topping on each breast, sprinkle with cilantro, and serve. FEEDS 6 TO 8

Crispy Chicken
with Lemon-Sesame BBQ Sauce

Skillet Cookin'

This dish perfectly combines the bright, bold flavors of Asian spices, fresh lemon, and BBQ sauce. All you've gotta do is fry up some chicken thighs and dress them in a tart, clingy sauce. The result is some powerfully provocative flavors. This sauce also works well with grilled chicken.

The Chicken
8 chicken thighs
Creole Seasoning (page 167)
Flour
Peanut oil for frying

The Sauce
2 tablespoons peanut oil
1 heaping tablespoon minced garlic
1 heaping tablespoon minced
    fresh ginger
2 tablespoons seeded and minced
    jalapeño pepper
⅓ cup soy sauce
1 to 2 teaspoons grated lemon zest
Juice of 1 lemon
¼ cup honey
1 tablespoon sesame oil
1 cup Mutha Sauce (page 165)
3 tablespoons toasted sesame seeds

Strip the skin from the chicken thighs and season lightly with Creole Seasoning. Toss them around in some flour, knocking off any excess. Pour ¼ inch of peanut oil in a heavy skillet and fire it up over medium-high heat til it's hot but not smoking. Fry the thighs til golden and cooked through, about 20 minutes. Flip them once after 10 minutes.

Get busy making the sauce while the chicken's cooking. Slap a small saucepan on the stove and add the peanut oil. Heat the oil over medium heat, and add the garlic, ginger, and jalapeños. Cook til the veggies are soft, then add the soy sauce, lemon zest, lemon juice, honey, sesame oil, and Mutha Sauce. Simmer for 5 minutes. Push the sauce off the direct heat, but keep it warm.

Check the chicken, and once it's done, take it out of the oil and let it drain briefly. Dip each piece in the sauce and arrange on a platter. Sprinkle the toasted sesame seeds over the chicken, and serve with any sauce that's left. FEEDS 4

))) **Always be deliberate.**
—Katherine Hepburn

Chicken Paprika
a.k.a. "The Thigh Master"

I'm very partial to chicken thighs, with their silky, succulent flesh. Slathered in a BBQ sauce spiked with good Hungarian paprika and made velvety with sour cream, this is a sensuous dish on a cold winter night, especially when served with buttered noodles to sop up all the good sauce.

The Chicken

3 pounds chicken thighs
Creole Seasoning (page 167)
½ cup olive oil
2 cups chopped onion
Pinch each of kosher salt and
　　black pepper
2 tablespoons minced garlic
¼ cup Hungarian paprika

1 cup Mutha Sauce (page 165)
2 ½ cups chicken broth or stock
　　(to make your own, see page 168)
1 ½ cups sour cream
½ cup sliced scallion

The Accoutrement

1 pound noodles, cooked and tossed
　　with plenty of butter

Strip the skin from the thighs, and season generously with Creole Seasoning.

Heat the oil over medium-high in a deep pan, and brown the thighs til golden, about 3 minutes on each side. It's better to cook the chicken in batches than to crowd the pan. Put the browned thighs on a plate.

Pour off all but 3 tablespoons of the oil, and slap the pan back on the heat. Throw in the onions, seasoning them with a pinch of salt and pepper, and cook til soft; then add the garlic and paprika and cook a few minutes longer. Stir in the Mutha Sauce and chicken broth and bring to a boil; put the chicken back in the pan, along with any juices left behind.

Cover the pan and lower the heat to medium-low. Simmer for 30 minutes, or til the chicken is done. Slowly add the sour cream to the sauce, stirring til well blended. Adjust the seasonings, adding more Creole Seasoning if you think it needs it. Stir in the scallions and serve with lots of buttered noodles.
FEEDS 4 TO 6

Failure is success if we learn from it.
—Malcolm Forbes

Chicken Steak Grandiose

Direct Grillin'

Just like the name says, this is a big chicken dish. Grilled whole boneless chicken breasts are layered with eggplant, prosciutto, basil, provolone, and BBQ sauce for a heaping meal-size portion. For those with dainty appetites, the same approach can be applied to half chicken breasts. You might even want to come up with your own grandiose combinations, like grilled zucchini, oregano, and feta; grilled portabella mushrooms, bacon, sautéed onions, and Cheddar; or grilled tomatoes, sliced sausage, chopped cilantro, and pepper-jack cheese. Remember, just think big.

2 medium eggplants
Kosher salt
¼ lemon
Creole Seasoning (page 167)
Olive oil
1 cup Mutha Sauce (page 165)

4 whole boneless, skinless chicken breasts (8 to 10 ounces each)
Coarsely ground black pepper
20 fresh basil leaves
¼ pound prosciutto, thinly sliced
6 slices provolone cheese

Peel the eggplants and cut into ½-inch rounds. Salt each round well. Layer them in a colander and let the slices drain for at least 30 minutes. Then give them a good squeezing between layers of paper towels. Squirt lemon juice over them and lightly sprinkle both sides with Creole Seasoning.

Build a medium coal bed in your grill. Brush the eggplant slices with oil, and grill for a couple of minutes on both sides, til tender, basting with some of the Mutha Sauce. Set the eggplant aside, but keep warm.

Cut slits in the top smooth side of the chicken breasts. Rub both sides with olive oil and season well with salt and pepper. Set aside.

Stack the basil leaves right on top of one another. Roll them up like a good cigar and slice them into thin ribbons. Set aside.

Open out the breasts butterfly fashion and place them on the grill with the slits up. Grill til golden, 5 to 6 minutes. Flip and grill til just cooked, about the same amount of time again. Brush the breasts with some of the Mutha Sauce. With the breasts still on the grill, cover them with slices of eggplant and most of the basil (reserve a bit for garnishing). Tear pieces of prosciutto to fit each breast, layer the pieces over the basil, and brush with some more of the Mutha Sauce. Top each with 1½ slices of provolone. Now you can close the lid of the grill and heat them til the cheese melts, or you can take the breasts off the grill and finish them under the broiler.

Sprinkle each portion with some of the remaining basil, and dig in.

FEEDS 4 (OR 8 IF HALF BREASTS ARE USED)

Oven-Roasted Mojito Chicken

Home cooking doesn't get any easier than this. So if you're serious about getting maximum flavor for a minimum amount of effort, this Cuban way of preparing chicken is for you. The onions and Mojito Marinade melt together into a tasty sauce that mingles well with some of our Perfect Rice.

The Chicken
1 chicken (3 ½ pounds), cut into
    8 pieces
1 cup Mojito Marinade (page 164)
1 large onion, sliced into ½ -inch rounds
2 tablespoons chopped fresh Italian
    parsley or cilantro

The Garnish
Lime wedges

The Accoutrement
Perfect Rice (page 117)

Spread the chicken out in a baking dish, and pour the Mojito Marinade over it. Get personal with the pieces and rub some of the marinade right up under the skin. Marinate the chicken for 4 hours, or overnight, in the fridge.

Turn the oven on to 375°. Scatter the onion slices over the bottom of a roasting pan, and put the chicken on top, skin side up. Pour the remaining marinade over the chicken and onions, and pop the pan into the oven. Roast for 1 hour and 15 minutes, til the chicken is golden and cooked through.

Lift the chicken pieces out of the pan and arrange them on a platter. Stir up the pan juices, adding a bit of fresh Mojito Marinade (if you have it) to wake up the flavors. Spoon the onions and pan juices over the chicken. Sprinkle with parsley or cilantro and garnish the dish with lime wedges. Get everybody to squeeze some lime over their portion for added flavor. Serve with Perfect Rice on the side.
FEEDS 4 TO 6

Chicken Vesuvio Dinosaur-Style

The last time I was in Chi-Town, I got the history of my favorite Chicago dish. It seems that the Italian immigrants who grew up in the shadow of Mount Vesuvio and then came to settle in Chicago developed this chicken and potato dish to celebrate the abundance of meat available in their new country, as well as their Neapolitan roots. We've given it a Dinosaur twist to get Vesuvio really smokin'.

3 large baking potatoes
Kosher salt and black pepper
2 ½ to 3 pounds chicken pieces
½ cup olive oil
10 large cloves garlic, minced
1 ⅓ cups dry marsala wine

Juice of 1 ½ lemons
1 cup Mutha Sauce (page 165)
1 ½ tablespoons dried oregano
¼ cup chopped fresh Italian parsley
10 ounces frozen peas, defrosted, cooked, and tossed with butter

Preheat the oven to 350°. Scrub the potatoes and cut each one lengthwise into 8 wedges, leaving the skin on. Season with salt and pepper and set aside.

Season the chicken with salt and pepper on both sides. Heat the oil in a large skillet set over medium-high. Cook the chicken for about 4 minutes on each side, and transfer to the biggest roasting pan you own.

Throw the potato wedges into the oil left in the skillet and cook them for 1 minute on each side. Remove the skillet from the heat and transfer the potatoes to the roasting pan with the chicken. If they don't all fit in a single layer, oil up another roasting pan and put the rest of the wedges in there.

Dump all but 2 tablespoons of the oil out of the skillet. Put it back on the heat and add the garlic. Cook for 1 minute and then stir in the marsala, lemon juice, Mutha Sauce, oregano, parsley, and salt and pepper to taste. Cook for 1 minute. Pour half of the sauce over the chicken and potatoes, saving the rest. Cover the roasting pan(s) with foil and bake for 30 minutes. Uncover and flip over the chicken and potatoes. Bake, uncovered, another 15 minutes. Flip the pieces again and pour the rest of the sauce over everything. Bake for 10 minutes more, til the chicken and potatoes are tender and glazed with the sauce.

Mound the chicken pieces in the center of a large platter. Then pile a ring of potato wedges around them, and scatter the peas over the top. Serve it hot and smokin'—just like a volcano.
FEEDS 6

Chicken-Fried Chicken

Skillet Cookin'

If you love good fried chicken, this is the quick version. It's just like its namesake, "chicken-fried steak." Breading up and frying a nice boneless flat piece of meat, whether it's beef or chicken, will give you a meal in minutes. It makes a great main course, or try slappin' the finished product in a crusty roll or even slicing it over a mess of salad greens.

The Chicken

2 ¼ pounds small boneless, skinless
    half chicken breasts
Sprinkling plus ¼ cup
    Creole Seasoning (page 167)
1 ½ cups buttermilk
2 cups flour

2 tablespoons kosher salt
Vegetable oil for frying

The Accoutrement

Cayenne Buttermilk Ranch Dressing
    (page 171)

Pull out the chicken tenders, if still attached, so you have a nice flat piece of meat. Sprinkle both sides of the breasts and tenders with Creole Seasoning. Line them up in a nonreactive baking pan and pour on the buttermilk. Cover and let marinate in the fridge for 4 hours or longer.

Mix up the flour, ¼ cup of Creole Seasoning, and the salt. Spread it out in a flat pan. Fish the chicken pieces out of the buttermilk, and press them into the flour mixture, coating them well all over.

Pour ¼ inch of oil in the bottom of a heavy skillet. Heat over medium-high til almost smoking. Add the chicken pieces without crowding the pan. Turn down the heat to medium and fry for about 5 minutes on each side. You might have to fry the chicken in 2 batches; if you do, keep the first batch warm in a 140° oven while you finish cooking. Serve hot, crisp, and golden with some Cayenne Buttermilk Ranch Dressing ladled over it. FEEDS 4 TO 6

Chicken with Andouille Sausage & Peppers

This is a variation on an old Italian dish called Chicken Scaparello, which is made with cut-up chicken, sausage, onions, and peppers simmered in a tomato sauce. Out of respect, we gave our version a different name and spiced the dish up a bit usin' sausages from Louisiana and a good dose of the Mutha Sauce. Either way it's good home cookin'. So make it yourself and eat hearty.

The Chicken

1 chicken (3 ½ pounds),
    cut into 8 pieces
Creole Seasoning (page 167)
½ cup olive oil
1 large red onion, chopped
1 large red bell pepper, cut into
    thin strips
Pinch each of kosher salt and
    black pepper
8 to 10 large cloves garlic, chopped
2 cups chicken broth or stock (to make
    your own, see page 168)

1 ½ cups Mutha Sauce (page 165)
3 bay leaves
4 to 5 pickled pepperoncini, cut
    in rounds
1 teaspoon dried thyme
⅓ cup red wine vinegar
¾ pound andouille sausage
2 tablespoons softened butter
¼ cup chopped fresh Italian parsley

The Accoutrement
Perfect Rice (page 117)

Spice up the chicken pieces by sprinkling Creole Seasoning all over them and rubbing it in for good flavor penetration. Pour the oil into a skillet set over medium-high heat. When it's hot but not smoking, add the chicken pieces and brown for 3 to 4 minutes on each side. Take them out and put them on a platter. Pour off all but 2 tablespoons of oil from the skillet.

Scoop up the onions and peppers and toss them into the remaining oil. Season with a pinch of salt and pepper and cook them, scraping up all the delicious browned bits of chicken clinging to the bottom of the pan. Cook for 3 to 4 minutes, til the veggies get soft. Add the garlic and cook for 1 minute more.

Douse the softened veggies with the broth and the Mutha Sauce. Toss in the bay leaves, pepperoncini, and thyme and pour in the vinegar. Give everything a good stir. Grab the chicken pieces and put them into the pan, skin side up. Bring to a simmer, partially cover, and let the ingredients simmer actively over medium heat for 20 minutes. While this is going on, slice the andouille sausage ½ inch thick and cook briefly in another skillet over medium heat to render out some of the fat. Take the slices out of the skillet and drain on paper towels. When the chicken has been simmering for 20 minutes, add the drained sausage to it, flip the chicken pieces so they're skin side down, and simmer for 15 minutes more.

Skim any oil from the surface of the sauce, fish out the bay leaves, and taste the sauce to see if you need to add a little more seasoning. Fold in the butter and parsley. Serve immediately on a bed of steaming Perfect Rice. FEEDS 4 TO 6

Chicken & Zucchini Piquante

This one-skillet dinner is loaded with flavor and easy to prepare. Serve over some steamin' Perfect Rice or your favorite macaroni. You can also substitute boneless, skinless chicken thighs for some real concentrated chicken flavor—love that dark meat!

The Chicken

1 ¾ to 2 pounds boneless, skinless
    chicken breasts
Sprinkling plus 2 teaspoons Creole
    Seasoning (page 167)
6 tablespoons olive oil
1 ½ cups chopped onion
1 cup chopped green pepper
1 cup sliced celery
Pinch each of kosher salt and
    black pepper
2 tablespoons chopped garlic
¾ cup Mutha Sauce (page 165)
1 can (28 ounces) diced
    tomatoes, drained

1 cup chicken broth or stock (to make
    your own, see page 168)
2 bay leaves
1 medium zucchini, quartered length-
    wise and cut into ½-inch slices
⅔ cup stuffed green olives, halved
2 teaspoons dried oregano
2 teaspoons ground cumin
1 teaspoon dried thyme
2 tablespoons sliced scallion

The Accoutrement

Perfect Rice (page 117) or
    cooked macaroni

Cut the chicken breasts into ¼-inch strips. Season them lightly with Creole Seasoning.

Fire up a large skillet over medium heat. Add the olive oil. When it's hot but not smoking, add the chicken strips and cook for a couple of minutes on each side, til lightly browned. With a slotted spoon, scoop the chicken out of the pan and onto a plate. Set aside.

Dump the onions, peppers, and celery into the oil left in the pan. Cook for about 5 minutes, til soft; then season with a pinch of salt and pepper. Add the garlic and cook for 1 minute more. Stir in the Mutha Sauce, tomatoes, broth, and bay leaves.

Cover and simmer for 8 minutes; take off the lid and simmer for 2 minutes more.

Toss in the zucchini, olives, oregano, cumin, and thyme. Simmer for 2 minutes. Slide the chicken strips back into the pan and cook for 5 minutes more. Taste and season with 2 teaspoons Creole Seasoning. Take out the bay leaves and stir in the scallions.

Lay down a bed of Perfect Rice or macaroni on each plate, and spoon the chicken mixture over it. Serve while it's pipin' hot. FEEDS 4 TO 6

Fish

BLUES
PLATE
SPECIAL

TODAY'S SPECIALS

GRILLED MANGO & COCONUT
SWORDFISH $14.95

POACHED SALMON IN
DILLED BBQ SAUCE $12.95

Clam, Shrimp, & Scallop Pan Roast

Shellfish lovers drool over the drunken-sweet richness of the sea infusing every inch of this dish. You can use clams, shrimp, and scallops as we do or substitute your own favorites—mussels, oysters, or even some firm-fleshed fish. Just be sure to serve the pan roast with a spoon and plenty of good bread to sop up all the tasty sauce.

The Shellfish

2 dozen littleneck clams

¼ cup olive oil

6 large cloves garlic, minced

1 cup clam juice

1 cup white wine

6 tablespoons Mutha Sauce (page 165)

1 teaspoon crushed red pepper

1 tablespoon Worcestershire sauce

½ to ¾ pound shrimp, in the shell
     (12 to 16 total)

½ pound sea scallops (preferably dry-packed)

1 tablespoon heavy cream

10 fresh basil leaves, chopped

The Garnish

2 tablespoons chopped fresh Italian parsley

Give the clams a good scrubbing, discarding any with cracked or open shells. Set aside. Heat the oil over medium-high in a pan that you can cover later. Throw in the garlic and cook for 2 minutes. Pour in the clam juice, wine, and Mutha Sauce. When the mixture is bubbling, add the clams. Cover and cook til the clams open, 3 to 5 minutes. Pull out the clams as they open, and keep them warm. (Pitch any clams that don't open.)

Boil and reduce the pan juices over high heat for about 8 minutes. Sprinkle in the red pepper and season up the sauce with Worcestershire.

Toss in the shrimp and scallops. Simmer til they're cooked and have just turned opaque, about 4 minutes. Swirl in the cream and basil. Return the clams to the pan, and gently stir together all the shellfish. Sprinkle with parsley and serve steaming hot. FEEDS 4

Direct Grillin'

Grilled Mango-Coconut
Swordfish

I never liked swordfish much til I had it sliced thin and flash-grilled. This keeps the flesh moist and succulent. You'll need to ask your fish seller for a piece of the swordfish loin so you can slice it yourself or have him do it for you. The difference in eating pleasure is worth the effort.

The Sauce

2 mangoes
2 tablespoons butter
1 jalapeño pepper, seeded and minced
1 tablespoon minced fresh ginger
Pinch plus 1 teaspoon kosher salt
Pinch of black pepper
¾ cup freshly squeezed orange juice
1 can (14 ounces) unsweetened coconut milk
    (see note)
3 tablespoons Mutha Sauce (page 165)

1 teaspoon grated orange zest
1 tablespoon finely diced red bell pepper
Juice of ¼ lime
Tabasco sauce

The Fish

1 whole loin of swordfish (2 ¾ pounds)
Olive oil
Creole Seasoning (page 167)

The Garnish

10 fresh basil leaves

Start with the sauce. Slice off the 2 ends of each mango. Stand them up on a cut end, and cut down close to the skin to peel it away. Slice the flesh away from the fibrous pit, and then dice the flesh. Toss the butter into a saucepan set over medium-high heat. Stir in the jalapeños and ginger with a pinch of salt and pepper and cook for 2 to 3 minutes, til soft. Add the mango and cook for 5 minutes more. Pour in the orange juice, coconut milk, and Mutha Sauce, and toss in 1 teaspoon salt. Turn the heat up to high and bring to a boil. Lower the heat to medium-high and simmer 15 minutes, til reduced by half. Keep warm. Just before serving, stir in the orange zest, peppers, lime juice, and Tabasco.

Wash the basil leaves, dry them, and stack them. Roll the leaves tightly like a good cigar, and cut across the roll into thin ribbons. Set aside.

Fire up the grill. Cut the skin from the swordfish, and cut the fish in half lengthwise along the grain. Flip each half onto its side and cut into ½-inch-thick steaks across the grain. Rub the steaks down with oil and season with a sprinkling of Creole Seasoning on both sides.

Clean the grill rack and oil it. Spread out a nice hot coal bed. Position the rack and throw the steaks onto it, directly over the coals. Cook for about 2 minutes and flip. Cook for another 1 to 3 minutes or so, til done but not overcooked. These babies should be succulent.

Arrange the steaks on a platter and spoon on the sauce. Dress them up with a sprinkling of basil.   FEEDS 5 TO 6

Note: Make sure you get coconut milk, not cream of coconut. The only ingredients listed on the can should be coconut milk and water.

Pan-Fried Cod
with Bacon-Fennel BBQ Sauce

Skillet Cookin'

This dish was created for a local fiery food show. It happened to be Lent at the time, so we figured fish would be a good seasonal choice. Then someone reminded us that the bacon was an unholy partner. With apologies to the Pope, we served it anyway because it was that sinfully good.

The Sauce

8 strips regular-slice bacon
1 heaping cup slivered red onion
1 heaping cup slivered fennel (see note)
Pinch each of kosher salt and black pepper
1 cup Mutha Sauce (page 165)
Juice of ¼ lemon

The Fish

½ cup flour
2 tablespoons Creole Seasoning (page 167)
Pinch of kosher salt
1 ½ pounds cod fillets, cut into 5-inch pieces
½ cup olive oil

The Garnish

3 tablespoons sliced scallion

Make up a batch of sauce. Fry the bacon over medium-high heat just til crisp and brown. Pull it out of the pan, drain it on paper towels, crumble, and set aside.

Pour off all but 3 to 4 tablespoons of the bacon fat in the pan. Dump in the onions and fennel, seasoning with a pinch of salt and pepper. Sizzle over medium heat til brown and caramelized. Stir in the Mutha Sauce and lemon juice. Keep warm.

Toss the flour, Creole Seasoning, and a pinch of salt together. Dredge the fish in the mixture til the pieces are well coated.

Swirl the oil into a heavy skillet and heat it til hot but not smoking. Knock the excess flour off the fish pieces, and slip them into the skillet. Cook for 2 to 3 minutes, til lightly browned. Flip the pieces over and cook another 2 to 3 minutes, til cooked through. With a slotted spatula, transfer the fish to a platter.

Top each portion with a spoonful of sauce, some bacon crumbles, and some sliced scallions. Serve it right away. FEEDS 4

Note: Fennel, sometimes called anise, is a bulbous vegetable with strings like celery and stalky tops tipped with feathery, aromatic leaves. It has a sweet licorice flavor that accents fish and poultry perfectly. The stalks are always removed, leaving just the bulbous bottom. Often you'll need to pull off the outer ribs if they look tough and fibrous. Then cut the bulb lengthwise in quarters. Wash well because sometimes sand gets lodged between the ribs. Cut out the core and discard; then sliver or slice the fennel.

Grill-Smoked Salmon
with Chile-Lime Booster Sauce

Cooter, our chef in Rochester, concocted this tongue-tinglin' booster sauce. Its flavor dances all around in your mouth with every tender bite of the sweetly smoked salmon.

The Sauce

1 ½ tablespoons olive oil
2 medium jalapeño peppers, seeded and minced
2 large cloves garlic, minced
⅔ cup rice wine vinegar
Juice of 1 lemon
Juice of 1 lime
1 ½ cups Mutha Sauce (page 165)
3 tablespoons honey
3 tablespoons chopped fresh mint

The Fish

3 large cloves garlic, minced
1 tablespoon minced fresh ginger
2 tablespoons brown sugar
½ tablespoon kosher salt
Black pepper
2 tablespoons olive oil
1 large salmon fillet (about 2 ½ pounds)

Douse 2 cups applewood chips with water to cover. Soak for half an hour. Remove the grill rack and fire up the grill.

Throw together the sauce. Heat the olive oil in a small saucepan over medium-high heat. Toss in the jalapeños and garlic. Cook for 2 minutes, then pour in the vinegar, lemon juice, and lime juice. Swirl in the Mutha Sauce, honey, and mint. Simmer briefly, then set the sauce aside and keep warm.

Crush the garlic and ginger to a paste along with the brown sugar, salt, and pepper. Work in the olive oil. Rub the mixture all over the pink flesh of the fish. Oil a piece of aluminum foil, and roll up the edges to make a pan for the fish. Place the fish on it, skin side down.

Check your grill. Once the coals are good and hot, push them off to one side. Drain the chips and scatter them over the coals. They'll splatter a bit and then start smoking nicely. Reposition the grill rack and place the fish in its pan on the side opposite the coals to cook with indirect heat. Cover the grill and smoke slowly at 250° to 275° for 40 to 45 minutes, till cooked through. Drizzle the sauce over the fish. Slice into portions and serve fast. FEEDS 6

 Skillet Cookin'

Poached Salmon
with Dill BBQ Sauce

We don't do much poachin' at the restaurant, but at home it's another story. This is how I like to fix salmon. It has a light, almost brothy BBQ sauce flavored with a bit of dill.

The Fish

2 boneless salmon fillets
    (8 to 10 ounces each)
Kosher salt and black pepper
2 tablespoons butter
3 large cloves garlic, minced
1 tablespoon minced fresh ginger
1 ½ cups dry white wine
1 cup water
½ cup Mutha Sauce (page 165)
6 sprigs dill

6 fresh sage leaves
1 tablespoon black peppercorns
½ tablespoon mustard seeds

The Sauce

1 tablespoon Dijon mustard
½ cup Mutha Sauce
1 tablespoon chopped fresh dill
Black pepper

The Garnish

Fresh dill sprigs

Season both sides of the salmon fillets with salt and pepper. Pick out a pan large enough to hold the salmon nice and tight in one layer. Toss the butter into the pan and melt it over medium heat. Add the garlic and ginger and let them sweat out their flavors for 2 minutes, being careful not to let them brown.

Pour in the wine, water, and the Mutha Sauce. Then toss in the dill, sage, peppercorns, and mustard seeds. Bring the mixture to a gentle boil. Immerse the salmon, skin side down. Bring the liquid back up to a bubbly boil for 30 seconds. Cover the pan loosely with a lid and turn the heat way down low.

Simmer for 10 to 15 minutes, til the fish begins to lightly flake. Gently lift the salmon out onto a plate, and keep it warm in a 140° oven.

Strain out the dill, sage, peppercorns, and mustard seeds, leaving just the poaching liquid in the pan. Turn the heat up to high and bring to a rapid boil. Reduce the liquid for 2 minutes. Make the sauce by whisking the mustard and Mutha Sauce into the poaching liquid. Add the dill and the pepper. Divide the salmon into 4 portions, placing each on a soup plate. Ladle the brothy sauce over each portion and garnish with a sprig of dill. Now enjoy the dancin' flavors of this simple dish.

FEEDS 4

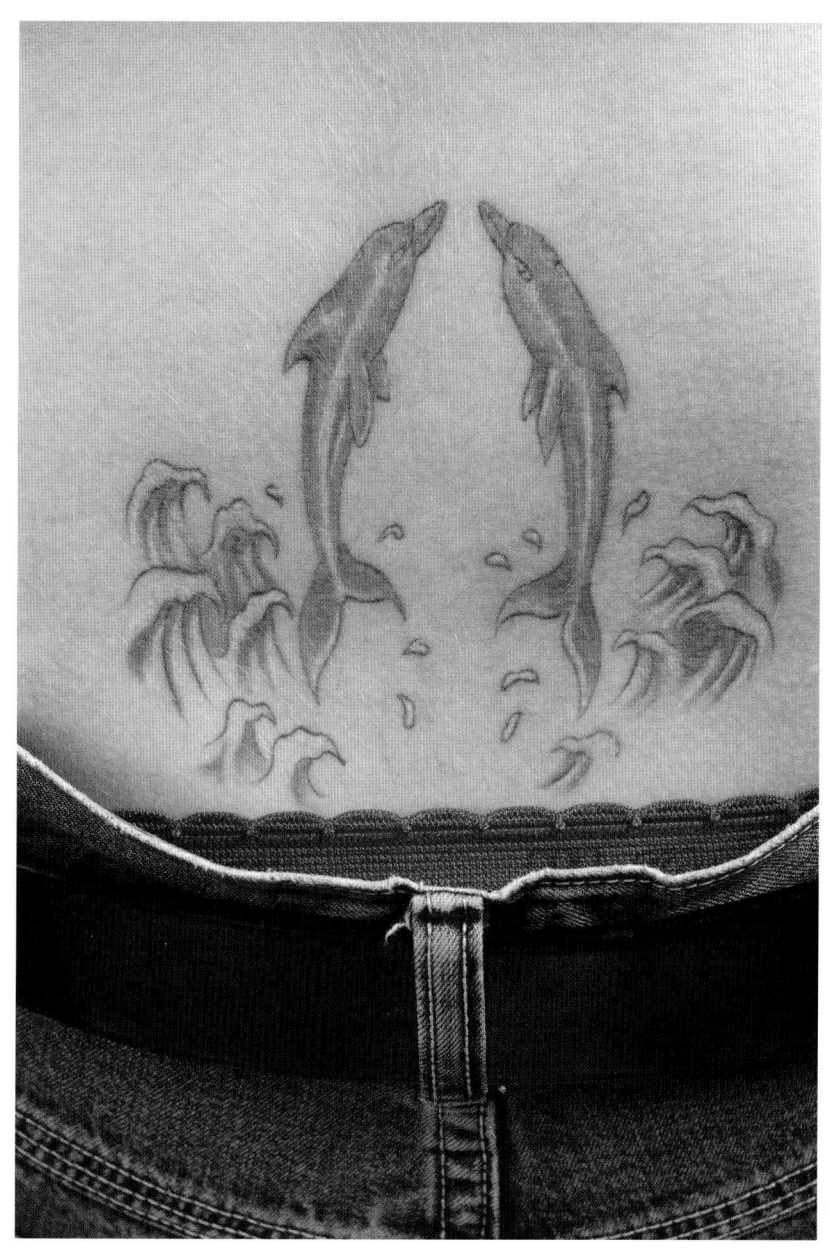

Sweet Potato-Crusted Mahi-Mahi
with Roasted Red Pepper Sauce

We think this is one fine fancy-pants dish. The sweet potato crust not only seals in the succulence of the fish but also gives it a crunchy, caramelized coating. The sauce of roasted red peppers simmered with lots of aromatics makes for a sexy finish.

The Sauce

2 red bell peppers
¼ cup olive oil
½ cup chopped red onion
1 shallot, peeled and minced
Pinch each of kosher salt and black pepper
2 tablespoons minced garlic
1 cup chicken broth or stock (to make your own, see page 168)
½ cup Mutha Sauce (page 165)
1 tablespoon heavy cream
Juice of ⅛ lemon

The Fish

4 mahi-mahi, tilapia, or other firm, white, ½-inch-thick fish fillets (about 1 ½ pounds)
Kosher salt and black pepper
¼ cup Creole mustard (preferably Zatarain's) or Dijon mustard
2 cups peeled, shredded yams or sweet potatoes
Coarsely ground black pepper
½ to ⅔ cup olive oil

Preheat the broiler. Line a small low-sided pan with aluminum foil. Set the peppers in it and stick the pan under the flaming hot broiler. Broil for 4 to 5 minutes on each side, til the skin blisters and blackens. Drop the peppers into a brown paper bag and seal them up for several minutes to let the steam loosen their skins. Pull the peppers out, peel, and remove the seeds. Dice the flesh and set aside.

Whip up the sauce. Fling a saucepan over medium-high heat. Pour in the oil and let it heat. Add the onions and shallots, seasoning with a pinch of salt and pepper. Cook til soft. Add the garlic and cook for 1 minute more before dumping in the peppers. Douse with the broth, Mutha Sauce, heavy cream, and lemon juice. Simmer 5 minutes, then transfer the steaming contents of the saucepan to a food processor. Whirl til smooth, and scrape the sauce back into the saucepan. Keep warm.

Inspect your fish fillets. If they have high spots, slice these down to get the thickness as even as possible. Season the fillets with salt and pepper, and spread the top side of each with 1 scant tablespoon of mustard.

Take handfuls of shredded potatoes and squeeze out the moisture. Press 4 to 5 tablespoons of shreds onto the top of each fillet so they stick to the mustard. Grind on lots of black pepper, and season with a pinch of salt.

Pour ½ cup of the oil into a nonstick frying pan. Set over medium heat til it sizzles when a drop of water is added. Cook 1 or 2 fillets at a time, potato side down first. Don't crowd the pan. Cook for 2 to 3 minutes, til the potatoes are nice and brown but not burned. Don't check til the fish has been cooking for at least 2 minutes. With a slotted spatula, carefully flip the fish over and cook for 2 to 4 minutes more, til cooked through. Remove from the pan and drain on paper towels while cooking the other fillets. Add more oil as necessary, but be sure it's nice and hot before adding more fish.

Ladle a puddle of sauce onto each of 4 plates. Nestle a fillet on top, and serve. FEEDS 4

Seared Tuna
with Wasabi Green Onion BBQ Sauce

Direct Grillin'

The tickle factor in this dish comes from the wasabi—Japanese horseradish. You can find it in the Asian section of your supermarket. And since we're cookin' in an Asian mode, we like the tuna served nice and rare, almost like sushi.

The Sauce
4 teaspoons wasabi powder
4 teaspoons plus ¼ cup water
2 tablespoons peanut oil
2 huge cloves garlic, chopped
1 tablespoon minced fresh ginger
Pinch each of kosher salt and black pepper
1 ¼ cups Mutha Sauce (page 165)
¼ cup soy sauce
1 tablespoon rice wine vinegar

½ teaspoon sesame oil
¾ cup sliced scallions, green part only

The Fish
4 tuna steaks, 1 ¼ to 1 ½ inches thick
    (about 1 ½ pounds total)
2 tablespoons olive oil
1 teaspoon five-spice powder
Kosher salt and black pepper

Make the sauce first. Dump the wasabi powder into a cup. Drizzle in 4 teaspoons of water, and mix to a paste. Set aside.

Set a small saucepan on the stove. Add the peanut oil and heat over medium-high. Toss in the garlic and ginger and season with a pinch of salt and pepper. Cook briefly, til barely soft. Swirl in the Mutha Sauce, soy sauce, vinegar, oil, and wasabi paste. Add the scallions and give everything a stir.

Scrape the sauce into a food processor and give it a spin for 5 seconds, or til smooth. Scrape back into the saucepan and add the remaining ¼ cup water. Mix and keep warm.

Rub the tuna steaks with olive oil. Sprinkle one side of the tuna steaks with half of the five-spice powder, some salt, and lots of pepper. Flip them and season the other side the same way.

Build a hot coal bed in your grill. Clean and oil the rack. Put the steaks on and cook for 2 minutes, til colored ⅜ inch up from the bottom. Flip and cook the same amount on the other side, leaving a nice rare streak through the center. The internal temperature will be around 100°.

Serve immediately with a generous spoonful of sauce over each steak. FEEDS 4

Lamb

Direct

Indirect
Grillin'

Butterflied Leg of Lamb
with Caramelized Onion BBQ Sauce

If you like to wow your friends with your backyard cooking prowess, this is one showboatin' dish you'll want to try out. I like what happens when you marinate lamb in yogurt. The enzyme action in the yogurt does something special to the meat, tenderizing it and giving it an exotic allure.

The Marinade

1 cup plain yogurt

Grated zest of 1 lemon

½ cup lemon juice

1 tablespoon olive oil

4 scallions, sliced

6 cloves garlic, chopped

¼ cup chopped fresh mint leaves

2 tablespoons dried thyme

2 tablespoons black pepper

1 tablespoon ground cumin

1 tablespoon kosher salt

The Lamb

1 leg of lamb, boned by a butcher (4 to 5 pounds boneless)

The Sauce

2 tablespoons butter

1 large onion, chopped

Pinch each of kosher salt and black pepper

1 cup chicken broth or stock (to make your own, see page 168)

1 cup Mutha Sauce (page 165)

1 teaspoon ground cumin

3 tablespoons chopped fresh mint

Make the marinade. Whirl all the marinade ingredients together in a food processor. Needle the lamb all over with a fork, and nestle it in a nonreactive bowl. Spoon the marinade onto the meat and slather it around til the meat is well coated. Cover and marinate in the fridge overnight.

Prepare a hot coal bed and mound the coals on one side of the grill. When you're ready to cook, scrape off all the marinade and pat the meat dry. Lay the lamb, boned side down, directly over the coals. Sear it for 4 minutes. Flip it over and sear the other side for another 3 to 4 minutes. Slide the meat away from the coals, to cook it with indirect heat. Cover the grill and adjust the heat so that it's 325° to 350° inside. Roast for 50 to 60 minutes, til the internal temperature reaches about 145°.

Get the sauce cooking while the meat roasts. Drop the butter in a saucepan and melt over low heat. Add the onions and season with salt and pepper. Cook slowly, stirring every now and then, til deeply caramelized. Add the broth, Mutha Sauce, and cumin. Keep warm over low heat.

Check the meat with an instant-read thermometer, and once it reaches 145°, pull it off the grill and let it rest for 15 minutes. Carve the lamb across the grain into ¼-inch slices on a cutting board with a well to catch all those delicious juices. You might have to remove some odd connectors or cut the muscle clods into more manageable sizes, but do what you've gotta do and keep carving across the grain. Arrange the meat on a platter.

Pour all the accumulated meat juices into the sauce, and boost the heat up for a minute or two to get it nice and hot. Stir in the mint and then ladle the sauce over the sliced lamb. It's ready to go.

FEEDS 6 TO 8

Note: Find a good butcher and make him your friend. He can make your life so much easier and get you better-quality meat than the ordinary stuff that comes in. Like everyone else, butchers respond to folks who show they care.

Lamb Shanks
Braised in Rosemary
Red Wine BBQ Sauce

I'm a big fan of anything braised, and these lamb shanks fit the bill. The fall-off-the-bone tenderness of the meat and the richness of the stock really turn me on. Served on a pile of grits, it's outstanding.

The Shanks

6 lamb shanks (about 4 ½ pounds)
Kosher salt and black pepper
⅓ cup plus ¼ cup olive oil
2 ½ cups chopped onion
3 tablespoons minced garlic
2 cups dry red wine

2 cups beef broth or stock (to make
　　your own, see page 169)
3 sprigs rosemary
1 cup Mutha Sauce (page 165)
½ cinnamon stick

The Accoutrement

Garlic & Cheddar Grits (page 126)

Preheat the oven to 350°. Grab a knife and make a couple of shallow slits through the silver skin on both sides of each shank. Sprinkle the meat on both sides with a generous amount of salt and pepper.

Schlepp a big, heavy frying pan over to the stove and heat it over medium-high. Pour in ⅓ cup olive oil and get it hot and fragrant. Add as many shanks as will fit comfortably in the pan without crowding, and cook til richly browned, about 4 minutes. Flip them over and brown the other side. Pull the shanks out and drop them in a roasting pan. Continue browning the rest of the shanks. Once all of them are done, clean out the pan and pour in the remaining ¼ cup olive oil.

Drag the pan back over medium-high heat and add the onions, seasoning them with salt and pepper. Cook til soft; then toss in the garlic and cook 1 minute more. Pour in the wine and broth and bring to a boil. Add the rosemary, Mutha Sauce, and cinnamon stick. Pour everything over the shanks and cover the roasting pan tightly with foil. Shove it in the oven to braise for 1 hour; then pull it out and give the shanks a flip. Pop them back in the oven to cook for another hour.

Once the shanks are tender and the meat is pulling away from the bone, lift them out onto a good-looking platter. Cover and keep warm. Strain the braising liquid, and skim the grease. Pour the braising liquid into a small pan and reduce by half. Keep warm.

Line up some dinner plates and mound a portion of Garlic & Cheddar Grits in the center of each one. Set a shank into each mound, spoon some of the sauce over each shank, and bring them to the table.　FEEDS 6

Direct Grillin'

Grilled Lemon-Pepper
Lamb Chops
with Rosemary-Dijon BBQ Sauce

This quick grill dish makes it easy to come home after work and eat well. The secret is in the simple sauce all seasoned up with the classic flavor partners that lamb loves the most—rosemary and Dijon mustard.

The Sauce

2 tablespoons butter
⅓ cup chopped shallot
Pinch each of kosher salt and
    black pepper
4 large cloves garlic, chopped
¾ cup red wine
1 sprig rosemary
¼ cup Dijon mustard
1 cup Mutha Sauce (page 165)

Juice of ¼ lemon
1 tablespoon honey
¼ cup sliced scallion

The Lamb

8 center-cut loin lamb chops
    (2 ½ to 3 pounds)
Olive oil
Lemon pepper

Fire up the grill. While that's heating, make the sauce. Toss the butter into a small saucepan and melt over medium heat. Add the shallots, season with salt and pepper, and cook til just wilted. Toss in the garlic and cook for 1 minute more.

Splash in the red wine and add the rosemary and mustard. Raise the heat to high, and reduce the sauce rapidly for 2 to 3 minutes. Mix in the Mutha Sauce, lemon juice, and honey and simmer for a minute or two to blend the flavors. Keep warm.

Rub the chops down with oil. Season both sides with a generous sprinkling of lemon pepper. Place over the coals. Cook for about 4 minutes, then flip the chops and cook for another 3 to 4 minutes, or til a rosy medium-rare, 130° to 135°. Pull them off the grill.

Fish out the rosemary sprig from the sauce, and stir in the scallions. Pour it over the chops and enjoy. FEEDS 4

Note: It's not unusual for the fat cooking off the edges of lamb chops to make the grill flare up. If this happens, cover the grill to choke off all the air. In a few seconds the flames will die down and you can uncover the grill again.

Rib Pit Boss Tips

It's pit boss time, so grab your matches, coals, hickory chips, foil, and beer 'cause you're gonna be a while. Patience is the key—there's no rushing good barbecue.

Meat Selection The ribs are the most important ingredient in this recipe. If they're not meaty, you'll be wondering why you spent so much time cooking bones. So get to know your butcher. He can steer you to a nice rack of ribs. You're gonna want one with a cap of meat covering the bones. You don't want to see any "shiners"—rib bones that have had all the meat scraped off them when the ribs were cut. At the restaurant we always get St. Louie racks, which are nice, even, rectangular racks, usually called 3 and down (which means they weigh 3 pounds or less). Cook the racks whole to keep them succulent, and then cut them up once they're done.

Smokin' Back in our pits we use quarter-split hickory logs to stoke our fires. However, for the home barbecue we've found that you can get great smoke penetration using hickory chips. You'll need to soak them in water before using in order to get 'em smokin'. Then you wrap the chips in aluminum foil, poking a few holes in the packets for the smoke to escape, rather than just scattering the chips on the coals. You'll need only about 3 cups of soaked chips divided into two packets to get the right smoke penetration for the ribs.

Low and Slow Slow and steady wins this race, so don't mess with the fire too much. And don't open and close the grill too often—about once an hour is plenty. Have an instant-read thermometer handy and check the grill's temperature by dropping the end of the thermometer through one of the vent holes. You want to keep the heat from 225° to 250°. If the temperature dips below 200°, add a few hot coals and keep cooking. If it gets too hot, just choke off the air vents a bit.

To Mop or Not to Mop In the world of serious barbecue, mopping ribs is always disputed. At the restaurant, we decide whether to mop based on which pit we're using, because the ribs are positioned in the pit in such a way that they are self-basting most of the time.

However, in the dry heat of the backyard grill, mopping ribs is a good idea. If the meat looks thirsty when you open the grill, you can mop 'em a little. Don't overdo it because you can kill your fire. When you mop ribs, don't brush them. This will disturb the crust that's forming. Instead, dab them lightly with the mop sauce.

Testing for Doneness Whether you cook ribs on the grill or in the oven, a 3-pound rack will take 3½ to 4 hours to get tender. Here's how to tell whether they're done: if you can gently tear the meat between the bones or poke your finger through it, or if the internal temperature is at least 180°, or if the ribs bend nicely when you grab them with a pair of tongs.

Finishing Touches There are two ways to finish ribs. You can glaze them or caramelize them. Glazing is a low-temperature method. After you've determined that the ribs have finished cooking, brush with BBQ sauce and let them cook for 20 minutes longer in the covered grill. To caramelize the ribs, crank the heat up to high on the grill and flip the finished ribs over onto direct high heat. (You can also do this under the direct heat of a broiler.) When they're nice and bronze colored, brush with BBQ sauce and serve.

Holding Ribs Once the ribs are glazed or caramelized, they can be held for up to 1 hour in a 140° oven, loosely wrapped in foil. Make sure the foil doesn't touch the glazed top of the ribs.

Servin' Ribs Let ribs, like any meat, rest for 5 to 10 minutes before slicing them into portions. At the Dinosaur we serve whole racks and half racks, letting our customers do the carving between the ribs. You can also cut them into individual ribs and serve them that way. Use a chef's knife or a cleaver to cut the meat between the bones. Make sure you give your guests lots of napkins and a couple of moist towel packets to clean themselves up after the feasting.

Dinosaur-Style Ribs

This is our reason for being. If you're a rib joint, you'd better have great ribs. What we strive for every day is a perfect balance of spice, smoke, sauce, and pull-off-the-bone tender pork. Here's the blueprint and some tips to achieve some beautiful barbecue. All you need are a few hours and a dedicated pit boss spirit. A couple of beers won't hurt either.

2 racks pork spareribs, St. Louie cut
(2½ to 3 pounds)
½ cup All-Purpose Red Rub (page 167)

Mop Sauce (page 164)
Mutha Sauce (page 165)

Read The Techniques of Outdoor Cookin' (page 12) and Rib Pit Boss Tips (page 92).

Pull off the grill rack and fire up the grill; then prepare the smoking packets by putting 3 cups of hickory wood chips in a bowl and covering them with water. Soak for at least half an hour. Drain well and divide between 2 squares of aluminum foil. Form into 2 individual packets, poking holes in one side. Set aside.

Get back inside to work on the ribs. Rub the ribs all over with the rub, making sure you are getting it into every surface. (You can even do this step well in advance.) Use just enough to coat the ribs evenly.

Spread out the coals once they're good and hot, piling them on one side of the bottom of the grill. Set the wood chip packets on top of the coals. Stick a drip pan filled with ½ inch of water on the side opposite the coals. This will catch the drips from the ribs and keep things moist inside the grill. Reposition the grill rack over the coals and the drip pan. Cover the grill and let the fire simmer down a bit.

Grab the ribs and position them on the rack over the drip pan. Cover the grill and test its internal temperature by dropping an instant-read thermometer down through a vent hole. You want the grill to be from 225° to 250°.

Walk away from the grill and let the heat and smoke do their thing. Come back to check on the ribs in about 45 minutes. Then check on things once every hour. If the ribs are looking a bit thirsty, mop lightly with the Mop Sauce. If the temperature of the grill is dipping below 225°, add a few more hot coals to the fire.

Test the ribs for doneness once they've been cooking for 3 ½ to 4 hours. You'll know they are done if you can gently tear the meat between the bones or poke your finger through the meat, or if they've reached an internal temperature of at least 180°, or if they bend nicely when you grab them in the middle with a pair of tongs. Once you've determined that they're done, get out the Mutha Sauce and pick a finishing touch from the two suggestions in the Rib Pit Boss Tips (page 92).

Pour another beer, then pull those tasty ribs off the grill, and you're ready to eat. FEEDS 2 TO 4

 **Oven Cookin'**

Cubano Mojito Oven-Roasted
Baby Back Ribs
with Habanero & Guava-Pineapple Tropical BBQ Sauce

Because our weather in Central New York is less than tropical, we have to figure out ways of keepin' those warm weather flavors coming even when poundin' rain or three-foot drifts make it hard to get to your backyard grill. So here's a way to make ribs in your oven and bring on all the flavors of places with better weather. Our method for makin' ribs in the oven can also be applied to the recipe for Dinosaur-Style Ribs (page 93). All you'll be missin' is the taste of the smoke and the smell of the outdoors, but the ribs will still be fallin'-off-the-bone tender.

The Ribs

2 racks pork baby back ribs
(2 ½ to 3 pounds)
1 cup Mojito Marinade plus more to use as a
mop sauce (page 164)
Black pepper

The Sauce

1 tablespoon vegetable oil

1 tablespoon minced ginger
1 teaspoon minced habanero pepper
2 cups diced fresh pineapple
6 tablespoons guava paste (see note)
¼ cup lime juice
2 tablespoons lemon juice
1 cup Mutha Sauce (page 165)
1 heaping tablespoon chopped
fresh cilantro

Set the ribs in a shallow roasting pan, and pour the Mojito Marinade over them. Flip the ribs around in it to make sure they're coated all over; then grind on lots of black pepper. Cover and marinate for 4 hours or overnight.

Preheat the oven to 250°. Put a wire rack over a jelly roll pan and pour 1 cup of water into the pan. Pull the ribs out of the marinade, scraping off any extra. Set the ribs on the rack, meaty side up. Slide them into the oven and roast slowly. Check every hour or so. If the meat looks dry, mop it lightly with some of the Mojito Marinade.

Cook up a batch of sauce while the ribs are roasting. Set a saucepan over medium-high heat. Pour in the oil, and once it gets hot, add the ginger and habanero peppers. Cook for 1 minute. Dump in the pineapple and the guava paste, stirring til the guava paste dissolves. Add the lime and lemon juices and the Mutha Sauce. Simmer for a couple of minutes to blend

the flavors. Stir in the cilantro. Set aside and heat up before serving.

Check the ribs for doneness after 2 ½ to 3 hours. They will be done if you can gently tear the meat between the bones or poke your finger through the meat, or if they've reached an internal temperature of at least 180°, or if they bend nicely when you grab them in the middle with a pair of tongs. Once they're tender, glaze the ribs with some of the sauce and keep cooking for 15 to 20 minutes. Or for a caramelized finish, turn on the broiler and get the surface of the ribs sizzling. When they're nicely bronzed, brush with the sauce.

Pull the ribs out and let them set for 5 to 10 minutes, then serve with the remaining sauce. FEEDS 2 TO 4

Note: Guava paste is found in the Hispanic foods section of your supermarket or in specialty stores carrying Hispanic foods.

Cookin' Perfect Pork

There was a time when folks cooked pork to death, bringing the internal temperature up as high as 185°. To a certain extent, you could get away with this 25 to 30 years ago because pork was a fattier meat back then and retained some natural succulence even when overcooked.

Today everything's changed about pork. It's safe, it's lean, it's even considered the "Other White Meat." The National Pork Producers Council recommends against overcooking pork. They have established 155° as their ideal internal temperature, which is right in the medium-well-done temperature range.

When I'm not slow cooking pork I still crave succulence, and so I prefer to cook pork just a bit less—to 145° or 150°, which is perfectly medium. The internal temperature of roasts and thick cuts will naturally rise by 5 to 10 degrees during the required resting time after you pull 'em from the oven or off the grill.

You should decide how you like your pork and cook it that way, now that you've got some opinions to consider.

Direct Grillin'

Apple-Brined
Double Cut Pork Chops
with Sausage & Corn Bread Stuffing

This is one of the best ways we know to use up day-old corn bread. We mix it with spicy Italian sausage and stuff it into some bodacious pork chops to turn out one good-lookin' dish for our Custom-Que menu.

The Pork
4 center-cut pork loin chops, 2 inches
      thick, with a pocket (14 to 16
      ounces each)
Olive oil
Black pepper
Mutha Sauce for basting (page 165)

The Stuffing
2 cups crumbled day-old corn bread
      (page 123)
3 tablespoons butter

1 cup chopped onion
¼ cup chopped red bell pepper
Sprinkling plus 1 teaspoon kosher salt
Sprinkling plus 1 teaspoon black pepper
2 large cloves garlic, minced
½ pound hot Italian sausage
2 tablespoons chopped fresh
      Italian parsley
¼ cup grated Pecorino Romano cheese
2 eggs, slightly beaten
2 teaspoons dried thyme

Brine chops 8 to 24 hours before cooking using the Apple-Brine recipe and instructions (page 98).

Fire up the grill and then make the stuffing. Dump the crumbled corn bread into a bowl and set aside. Grab a skillet and melt the butter in it over medium-high heat. Toss in the onions and peppers and season with salt and pepper. Cook til soft, then toss in the garlic and cook for 1 minute more. Strip the casing off the sausage and crumble it into the skillet. Cook til it loses its pink color, chopping and stirring constantly to break up the pieces. Scrape it all into the corn bread. Mix in the parsley, Pecorino Romano, and eggs and season it all with thyme, 1 teaspoon salt, and 1 teaspoon pepper.

Take the chops out of the brine and dry them off. Push 3 large pinches of stuffing into the pocket of each chop. Really stuff it in there tightly, filling it nice and full. Brush the chops with olive oil and season both sides with pepper.

See how the grill's doing. Pile the coals to one side. Sear the chops directly over the coals, 3 to 4 minutes per side. Be careful not to overcook them at this point, because it will make them curl up.

Slide the chops to the other side of the grill, away from the coals. Cover the grill and adjust the heat so that it's about 350° inside. Cook the chops for 45 to 50 minutes. Take their temperature by inserting an instant-read thermometer horizontally into the meat, parallel to and close to the bone without touching it. When it reads 145°, baste the chops with the Mutha Sauce. Cover the grill again and continue cooking for another 10 minutes, or til the internal meat temperature reaches 150° (see Cookin' Perfect Pork, page 95).

Pull those plump babies off the grill and eat 'em up without delay.   FEEDS 4

Brining Pork Chops

The new leaner style pork is missing something—fat. That great old conveyor of flavor and succulence has been bred right out of the loin meat of my favorite critter. Lean meat may be healthier, but I found that eating a pork chop was just not worth tiring my jaws out. That changed when I got turned on to brining. During the process the protein strands in the meat unwind and then get tangled up with other unwound strands, allowing them to trap moisture inside these new little webs. This results in juicier meat with better texture after cooking. Things get even better if you add some sugar to the brine, which boosts the caramelized flavor of the grilled surface of the meat. Give it a try and see for yourself how adding a brining step to your pork prep will have you lickin' your chops again.

Apple-Brine
(makes enough for 4 to 6 pounds of pork)
1 quart water
1 quart apple juice
½ cup kosher salt
1 cup maple syrup

1 ½ teaspoons thyme
1 ½ teaspoons black peppercorns
3 bay leaves
3 cloves garlic, crushed
1 jalapeño pepper, sliced in half and seeded
2 tablespoons apple cider vinegar

Dump all the ingredients into a large saucepan and bring to a boil over high heat. Boil for 15 minutes. Strain the brine into a bowl, cool to room temperature, and then chill completely in the refrigerator before using.

Add chops to the brine and let them marinate in the refrigerator for 8 to 12 hours. Pull them out and dry them off before using in a recipe.

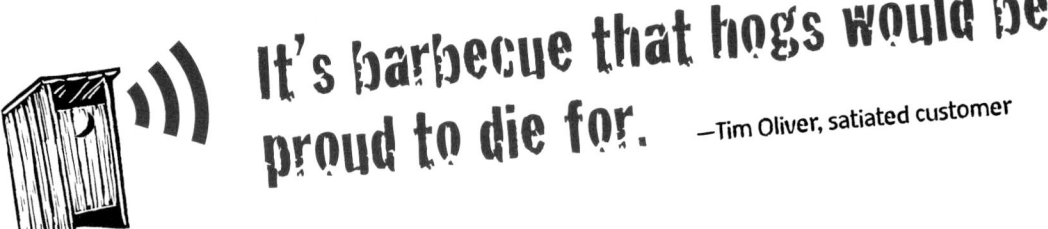

It's barbecue that hogs would be proud to die for. —Tim Oliver, satiated customer

Jerked Pork Tenderloins

Direct Grillin'

Here's an interesting technique. We cut (counter to logic) the pork tenderloins into long steaks along the grain of the meat, forming steaks approximately 10 inches long by 2 inches wide. Whip up the jerk paste the night before or that morning, and get the tenderloins marinating early. That way you can grill and eat in minutes after getting jerked around at work all day.

The Paste

1 large onion, cut in 16 pieces
2 large jalapeño peppers, stems and
    seeds removed
2 large cloves garlic
1 medium bunch scallions, white parts
    plus 4 inches of green, sliced
2 teaspoons dried thyme
1 teaspoon ground allspice
1/4 teaspoon ground nutmeg
1 teaspoon ground cinnamon
1 tablespoon kosher salt
1 teaspoon black pepper

1 tablespoon brown sugar
1 tablespoon olive oil
1/4 cup soy sauce
Juice of 1/2 lime

The Pork

4 pork tenderloins
    (about 2 3/4 pounds)

The Sauce

1/2 cup reserved jerk paste
1 cup Mutha Sauce (page 165)
1/3 cup water

Throw all the jerk paste ingredients into a food processor. Start by processing with on/off pulses, scraping the workbowl down several times. Then continue processing to a paste. Set aside.

Slice each tenderloin lengthwise along the grain into 3 even slices. Pound each slice lightly with the edge of a mallet to make indentations on both sides without opening holes in the meat.

Save 1/2 cup of jerk paste for the sauce. Place the tenderloins in a nonreactive pan and rub the remaining jerk paste into all sides. Cover and marinate in the fridge for at least 4 hours or all day, if possible.

Fire up the grill good and hot. Throw all the ingredients for the sauce into a small saucepan and bring the mixture to a gentle simmer. Let it bubble for 15 minutes. Keep warm.

Scrape off most of the jerk paste from the meat so it doesn't stew on the grill. Place the tenderloin slices directly over the coals and grill til the meat reaches an internal temperature of 145° to 150° (see Cookin' Perfect Pork, page 95), 4 to 5 minutes on each side.

Take the tenderloins off the grill, cut them into serving-size pieces, and pass them around with lots of sauce.
FEEDS 6 TO 8

Pan-Fried Pork Medallions
with Creole Honey-Mustard Sauce

It doesn't get much easier than this—or tastier. That wonderful Zatarain's Creole Mustard (see Resources, page 175) is hard at work for you, makin' an easy sweet and savory sauce that brings out the best in pork.

The Sauce

2 tablespoons butter

5 large cloves garlic, chopped

Pinch of kosher salt

1 cup Creole mustard (preferably
    Zatarain's) or spicy brown mustard

½ cup white wine

1 cup Mutha Sauce (page 165)

3 tablespoons honey

1 teaspoon Creole Seasoning (page 167)

The Pork

1 boneless center-cut pork loin roast
    (2 to 2 ½ pounds)

Creole Seasoning

½ cup vegetable oil

Start with the sauce. Melt 1 tablespoon of the butter in a small saucepan over medium heat. Toss in the garlic with a pinch of salt. Cook for 1 minute, just to soften it a bit. Add the mustard, wine, Mutha Sauce, honey, and Creole Seasoning. Turn the heat down to low and simmer for 10 minutes. Keep warm on a back burner.

Sharpen your knife and slice the pork loin into ¾-inch medallions. You should get about 10. Season liberally on both sides with Creole Seasoning.

Drag a large cast-iron skillet over to the stove and turn the heat up to high. Heat the pan til smoking hot, about 10 minutes. Pour in the oil and heat for about 30 seconds. Add a few medallions—don't crowd the pan—and cook for 2 to 3 minutes on each side. Take them out and put them on a platter. Keep warm while you cook the rest of the medallions.

Swirl the remaining 1 tablespoon of butter into the warm sauce. Serve these tasty medallions with some of the sauce spooned over each one. Any sauce that's left can be passed for ladling at the table.   FEEDS 4 TO 5

Apple-Maple Roasted Pork Loin

Come fall in Central New York, there's nothing that clears your head better than a motorcycle ride through the countryside bustin' with apple orchards and flamin' with red sugar-maple trees. So it just comes naturally for us to combine apples, maple syrup, and barbecue.

The Pork
1 pork loin with the rib bones attached
    (3 ½ to 4 pounds)

The Rub
1 tablespoon kosher salt
1 tablespoon brown sugar
1 tablespoon freshly cracked
    black pepper
Pinch of cayenne pepper
3 tablespoons olive oil

The Sauce
¼ cup butter
1 tablespoon minced garlic
1 jalapeño pepper, seeded and minced
Pinch each of kosher salt and
    black pepper
1 pound McIntosh apples, peeled,
    cored, and diced
¾ cup pure maple syrup
½ teaspoon ground cinnamon
⅛ teaspoon ground allspice
¾ cup Mutha Sauce (page 165)
¼ cup water

The Garnish
3 tablespoons sliced scallion

Preheat the oven to 500°. Get the butcher to cut the chine bone from the roast for easy carving later. Mix up all the ingredients for the rub, and massage it all over the roast. Place the roast, rib side down, in a roasting pan and pop it in the oven. Cook for 30 to 40 minutes to caramelize the outside, then lower the heat to 350° and continue roasting slowly for another 25 to 30 minutes, til the internal temperature registers 150° (see Cookin' Perfect Pork, page 95).

Throw together the sauce while the pork is roasting. Melt the butter in a saucepan. Toss in the garlic and jalapeños with a pinch of salt and pepper, cooking til soft. Dump in the apples and give them a stir. Cook til soft but not mushy, 8 to 10 minutes. Add the maple syrup, cinnamon, allspice, Mutha Sauce, and water, and simmer gently for 15 minutes. Keep warm.

Take the roast out of the oven and let it rest for 15 minutes. Slice the meat between the ribs into chops. Pour any meat juices that ooze out while carving into the sauce and stir it up a bit. Ladle some sauce onto each chop and sprinkle with scallions. Serve 'em up and pass the remaining sauce at the table.

FEEDS 6

Roasted Garlic & Chile-Crusted Pork Loin

This dish has some serious garlic happenin'. We developed it as one of a whole bunch of recipes for a Dinosaur garlic festival. It marked the birth of the Custom-Que at the restaurant, a special menu that's broadened our repertoire and given our customers a taste of some unique dishes influenced by the world of wood-fired cookin'.

The Rub

2 bulbs Roasted Garlic (page 170)
1 tablespoon kosher salt
2 teaspoons ground ancho chile
2 teaspoons dried flaked chipotle chile
1 teaspoon ground cumin
2 teaspoons brown sugar
1 tablespoon olive oil

The Roast

1 boneless double pork loin roast
(about 3 pounds)
4 large cloves garlic, quartered
Kosher salt and black pepper

Squeeze the roasted garlic pulp from each clove into a bowl. Add the salt, ground and flaked chiles, cumin, brown sugar, and olive oil and make a wet rub.

Stab holes into the pork loin and insert a quarter of a garlic clove into each. Massage the wet rub all over the meat, pushing some of it in between the two loins. Do this ahead, cover, and refrigerate overnight for maximum flavor penetration.

Fire up the grill, mounding a hot coal bed on one side. Just before grilling, season the meat all over with salt and a grinding of black pepper.

Set the meat directly over the coals to sear for 2 minutes, making sure to scrape onto the roast any of the coating rub stuck to the plate it was setting on. Sear the remaining 3 sides for 2 minutes each. Push the meat to the other side of the grill, away from the coals. Cover the grill and adjust the heat so that it's from 325° to 350° inside. Roast for about 1 hour, til the meat reaches an internal temperature of 150° (see Cookin' Perfect Pork, page 95). Pull the roast off the grill and let it rest for 15 minutes.

Carve and serve immediately, or let it cool completely and then slice for sandwiches. FEEDS 6

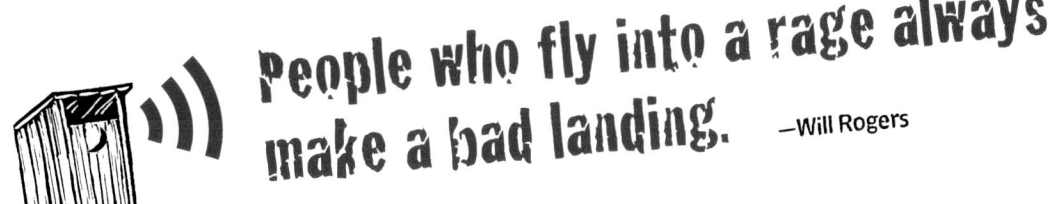

People who fly into a rage always make a bad landing. —Will Rogers

Home-Style Pulled Bar-B-Que Pork

Pulled pork is one of the wonders of true blue barbecue. It starts with a pork butt, also called a Boston butt, which is the meat surrounding the shoulder blade of the pig. This is a tough, fatty piece that's magically transformed with spices, smoke, and slow cookin' into something lean and melt-in-your-mouth tender.

1 ½ to 2 tablespoons vegetable oil
6 to 8 tablespoons All-Purpose Red Rub
(page 167)

1 pork Boston butt shoulder (6 to 7 pounds)
2 cups Mutha Sauce (page 165)

Check out the instructions in The Techniques of Outdoor Cookin' (page 12).

Dump 9 cups of hickory wood chips in a bowl, cover with water, and let them soak for half an hour or so. Drain and divide them between 6 squares of aluminum foil. Wrap up into individual packets, poking holes in the top. Set aside.

Pull off the grill rack and fire up the grill. While that's going on, mix together the oil and the rub. Rub this all over the pork butt. Once the coals are good and hot, pile them up on one side of the bottom of the grill and set 2 of the wood chip packets right on the coals. Position a drip pan filled with ½ inch of water on the side opposite the coals. Put the grill rack back in place. Set the pork butt, fat side up, over the drip pan, and close the lid. After about half an hour, check the grill temperature. It should settle down to 225° to 250°. If it's hotter, close down the vent holes. If it's cooler, open them up a bit.

Check the temperature of the grill every hour for the next 7 to 8 hours and make adjustments. If the temperature dips down to 200° or less, add a couple of hot new briquettes to the pile of gray coals, close the lid, and open the vent holes a bit.

Reach into the grill with some tongs after the pork butt's been smoking for 1 ½ hours, and remove the old packets of wood chips. Toss two new packets of foil-wrapped chips onto the coals. Repeat after another 1 ½ hours.

After the pork butt's been on the grill for 4 to 5 hours, you have achieved the necessary smoke penetration. It should be a rich mahogany brown, and the internal temperature should be about 155°. Grab the meat with tongs, remove it from the grill, and wrap it tightly in foil. Put the foil-wrapped pork butt back over the drip pan and cover the grill. Now you're sealing in the succulence of the meat as you continue to cook. This will take another 3 to 3 ½ hours. So keep working to maintain an even temperature of 225° to 250°. The pork is done when you can push down on the foil and it doesn't spring back or when you can pull out the shoulder blade bone easily without very much resistance.

Lift the foil-wrapped pork butt off the grill and let it rest (still covered in foil) for 10 to 15 minutes. Open the foil and strip off the fat cap on top of the meat, and then pull out the shoulder blade (if you haven't already). Carefully pull the meat apart, removing any visible fat and connective tissue. Shred the meat by squishing it between your fingers—the dark meat will shred easily, but you might have to pull apart the whiter meat into strings.

Put the pulled pork into a baking pan and pour the Mutha Sauce over it. Use it right away, or cover it with foil and rewarm in a 200° oven. Now it's ready to pack into rolls for sandwiches. Be sure to serve some more Mutha Sauce at the table. FEEDS 8

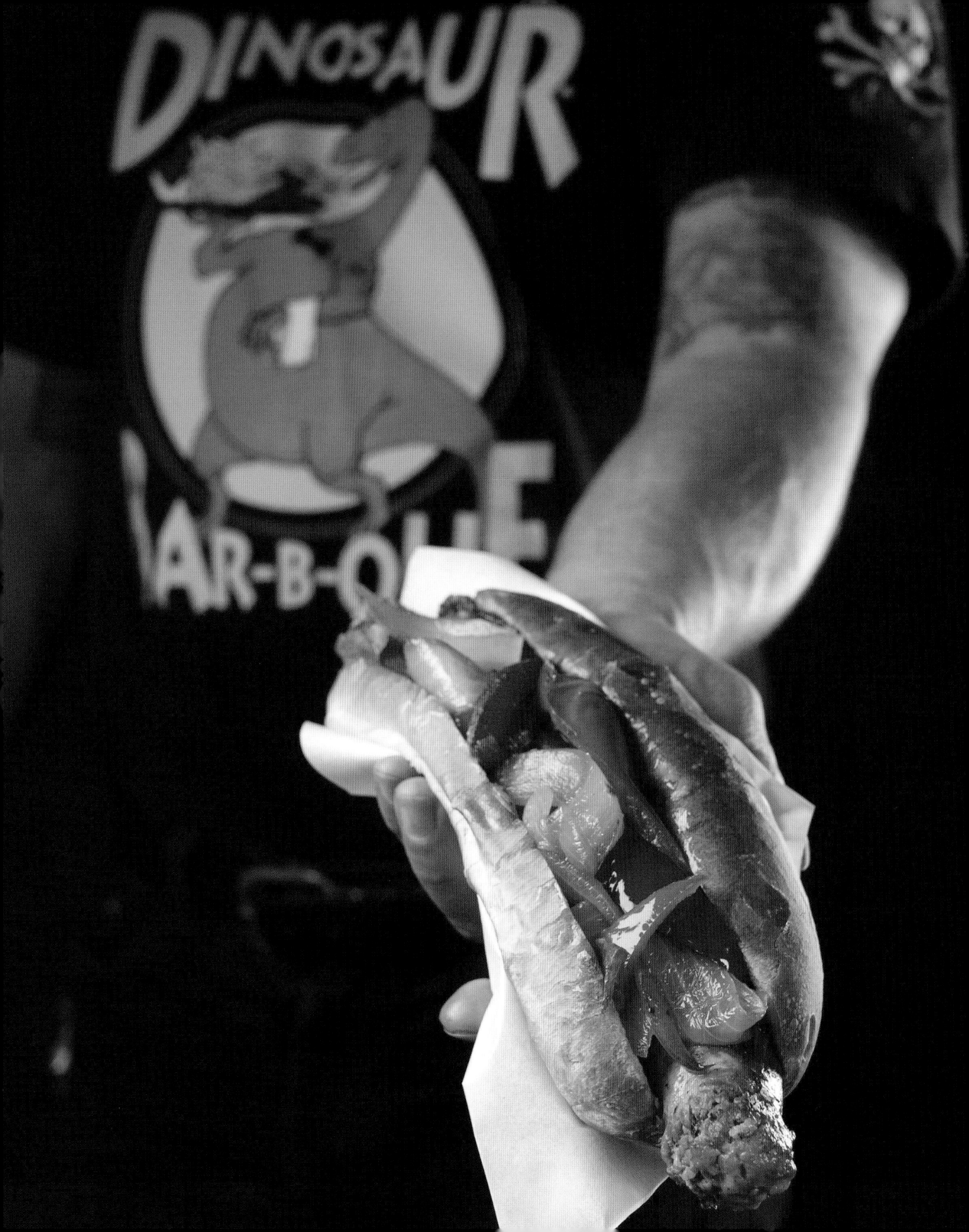

State Fair
Sausage & Pepper Sandwich

Skillet Cookin'

"How 'bout a nice sausage sandwich?" From 1983 to 1988 my partner, Mike, and I belted that line out thousands of times at fairs and festivals up and down the East Coast. Those were the days of Dinosaur Concessions, when we made our living slingin' sausage and charbroilin' steak for sandwiches. We pretty much retired from the fair business in 1988 when we opened the Dinosaur Bar-B-Que. But ten years later we were back at it again. In 1998 we joined forces with Steve Davis from Gianelli Sausage, whose family stand has been a mainstay at the New York State Fair for as long as I can remember. Gianelli (see Resources, page 175) makes a great sausage—lean, yet packed with flavor—just great for our State Fair Sausage & Pepper Sandwich and all our other sausage specialties.

2 tablespoons plus ¼ cup olive oil
1 ½ large onions, sliced into thick strips
1 large red bell pepper, sliced into thick strips
1 large green pepper, sliced into thick strips

Kosher salt and black pepper
2 pounds Italian sausage, hot or sweet
6 crusty submarine rolls

Slap 2 skillets on the stove. Put 2 tablespoons of olive oil in one and ¼ cup olive oil in the other. Dump the onions and peppers into the one with less oil and cook over medium-high heat, seasoning with salt and pepper. Heat the skillet with the larger amount of oil over medium heat for several minutes. Slide the sausages into the pan.

Cook for 15 minutes, or til they just lose their pinkness inside. Pull the sausages out of the pan and nestle them into the peppers and onions.

Slice up the rolls and stuff them full with sausages and peppers. Serve 'em up nice and hot with lots of napkins. FEEDS 6

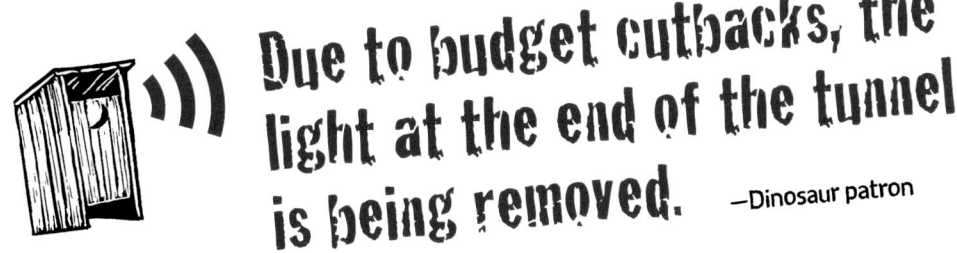

Due to budget cutbacks, the light at the end of the tunnel is being removed. —Dinosaur patron

Grilled Pork Chops
with Brandied Peach BBQ Sauce

Direct Grillin'

When the peaches are perfect, ripe and succulent, make this dish. The real fun comes when you set the sauce ablaze. Just watch your eyebrows!

The Chops
4 bone-in center loin pork chops
2 tablespoons Creole Seasoning
    (page 167)
2 tablespoons olive oil

The Sauce
1 pound fresh peaches (or use frozen
    if peaches are not in season)

¼ cup butter
1 tablespoon minced fresh ginger
1 tablespoon brown sugar
¼ cup brandy
½ cup Mutha Sauce (page 165)
⅛ teaspoon ground cinnamon
Kosher salt and black pepper

Fire up the grill and get it nice and hot while you do some cooking inside.

Slit the bootstrap tendon on the side of each chop (if there is one) in one place so the chops won't curl on the grill. Mix up a paste of the Creole Seasoning and oil. Rub this generously into the chops. Set aside.

Get busy with the sauce. Slit the skin of the peaches on the bottom with an X, then plunge them into boiling water for 30 seconds. Remove, peel, and cut in half. Pluck out the pits, and slice the peaches up lengthwise.

Drop the butter into a saucepan set over medium heat. Once it melts, add the ginger and cook til soft. Slide in the peach slices and brown sugar and give it all a gentle stir. Pour in the brandy and ignite with a match. Once the flame dies down, add the Mutha Sauce and cinnamon and season with salt and pepper.

Get out and check your grill. If you're using charcoal, spread a nice even coal bed and set the chops directly over the coals. When the juices rise up to the surface near the bone, give the chops a flip. Continue cooking til the meat reaches an internal temperature of 145° to 150° (see Cookin' Perfect Pork, page 95). All in all, the chops should be done in 8 to 10 minutes. Don't overcook them.

Serve 'em up on a platter with the sauce spooned all over. FEEDS 4

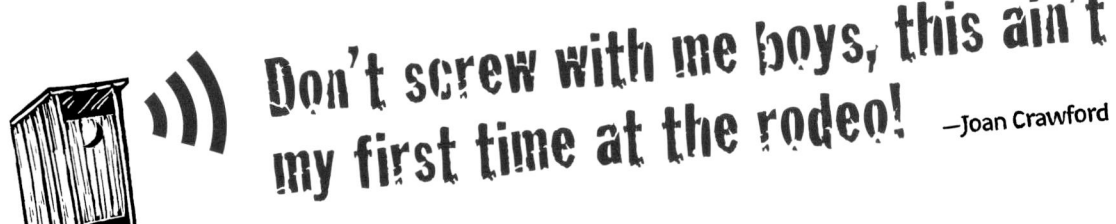

Don't screw with me boys, this ain't my first time at the rodeo! —Joan Crawford

Sides

Asparagus, Red Pepper, & Potato Salad

When spring hits and the asparagus comes into season, I can't wait to eat this simple potato salad. Because it's made without mayonnaise, it can be held at room temperature where the flavors can really develop. It's perfect picnic food. Once the asparagus goes out of season, try making it with a pound of green beans instead.

The Veggies
1 pound new red potatoes
1 pound asparagus
½ large red bell pepper, seeded
½ cup slivered red onion

The Dressing
5 tablespoons Creole mustard
(preferably Zatarain's) or spicy
brown mustard

6 tablespoons balsamic vinegar
1 ½ tablespoons brown sugar
¾ teaspoon kosher salt
¼ teaspoon black pepper
1 clove garlic, pressed or finely minced
6 tablespoons olive oil
Tabasco sauce

Scrub the potatoes and cook in boiling salted water to cover til tender. Without peeling, cut the potatoes into ¾-inch cubes and put them into a bowl. Snap off the tough bottoms of the stalks of asparagus and discard, then cook the tender tops in a shallow pan of simmering salted water til tender-crisp. Drain and shock in cold water. Slice the asparagus into 1 ½-inch pieces and add to the potatoes. Cut the pepper into sticks about the same width and length as the asparagus. Put in the bowl. Add the red onion.

Mix up some dressing by stirring together the mustard, vinegar, brown sugar, salt, pepper, and garlic in a small bowl. Drizzle in the oil, whisking constantly to make a creamy dressing. Add a couple of dashes of Tabasco to boost the flavor to your liking.

Splash the dressing onto the vegetables and give the salad a good stir. Serve right away for best color in the asparagus. FEEDS 5 TO 6

Mark Wenner of the Nighthawks

Creole Potato Salad

We make this salad every Sunday at the restaurant. I like to cook the potatoes til they're soft so the dressing can penetrate deeply. But the true secret to our potato salad is the Zatarain's mustard we have shipped up from New Orleans (see Resources, page 175). Sure, you can use another coarse-grain mustard, but once you've had a real Creole mustard, nothing else will give you satisfaction.

The Salad
2 pounds red potatoes
4 hard-cooked eggs, peeled
    and chopped
½ cup minced red onion
1 cup diced celery
4 cloves garlic, minced
2 teaspoons Creole Seasoning (page 167)
2 teaspoons kosher salt
1 teaspoon black pepper

The Dressing
1 cup mayonnaise
½ cup Creole mustard (preferably
    Zatarain's) or spicy brown mustard
1 teaspoon brown sugar

The Garnish
4 strips cooked bacon, crumbled (optional)

Drop the potatoes in a pot of well-salted boiling water. Cook til a fork pierces their tender flesh easily. Drain and cut the potatoes into 1-inch chunks, then throw them together in a large bowl with the eggs, onions, celery, garlic, Creole Seasoning, salt, and pepper.

Make the dressing by whisking up the mayonnaise with the mustard and brown sugar. Pour over the potatoes and give everything a good stir. Taste for seasoning and add salt and Creole Seasoning if it needs it.

Crumble the bacon on top right before serving.
FEEDS 6

Macaroni Salad

Here's a classic side dish if there ever was one. There's a thousand ways to make it, and I think you'll find ours to be a keeper—Creole mustard, fresh diced tomato, and a touch of green pepper all tossed with freshly cooked pasta shells. We like the way shells hold the dressing better than elbows. It's still Macaroni Salad to us.

The Salad
1 pound small pasta shells
2 medium ripe tomatoes, cored and diced
1 cup thinly sliced celery
½ cup finely diced green pepper

The Dressing
1 cup mayonnaise
¼ cup Creole mustard (preferably Zatarain's)
or spicy brown mustard
4 cloves garlic, minced
1 teaspoon brown sugar
1 teaspoon kosher salt
1 teaspoon black pepper

Cook the shells in a large quantity of well-salted, rapidly boiling water til al dente. Drain and cool down the shells under cold running water. Drain again and put them in a large bowl. Add the tomatoes, celery, and peppers.

Make the dressing by mixing up the mayonnaise, mustard, garlic, sugar, salt, and pepper. Stir into the pasta til coated and creamy. Taste and fix the seasonings if you need to. Refrigerate or serve pronto. FEEDS 8

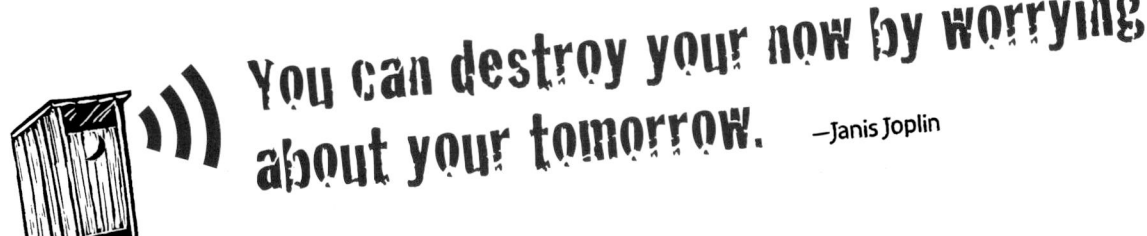

You can destroy your now by worrying about your tomorrow. —Janis Joplin

Coleslaw

Coleslaw is an absolute essential in a barbecue joint. We make ours fresh twice a day so the crispness and integrity of the cabbage always contrasts with the tangy, creamy dressing. What I'm saying is, it don't get better with age.

The Veggies
1 cabbage (2 ½ to 3 pounds)
2 or 3 carrots, peeled and shredded

The Dressing
2 cups mayonnaise
1 cup cider vinegar

1 tablespoon minced garlic
1 tablespoon brown sugar
¼ large onion, grated
1 tablespoon kosher salt
1 tablespoon black pepper
1 teaspoon celery seed

Cut the cabbage in quarters through the stem end. Cut out the core, and slice each quarter across the grain into ¼-inch slices. Then cut crosswise across the slices in 3 or 4 places to give you strips about ¼ inch wide by 2 inches long. You'll need about 11 cups. Toss the cabbage in a large bowl together with the shredded carrot.

Whip up the dressing. Throw all of the dressing ingredients together in a bowl and mix real well. If the cabbage is young, fold the dressing into it just before serving; if it's older, you can add it and hold the salad for several hours in the fridge.   FEEDS 8 TO 12

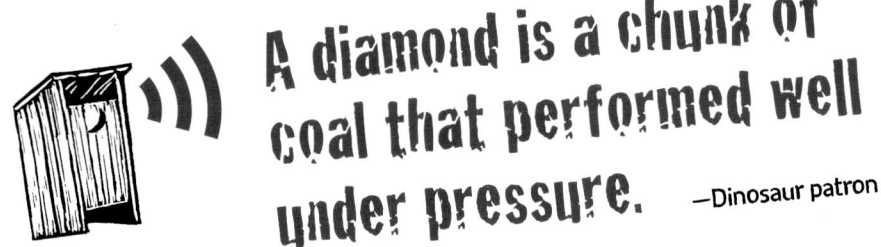

A diamond is a chunk of coal that performed well under pressure. —Dinosaur patron

Tomato-Cucumber Salad

This recipe was inspired by an Italian recipe handed down by my partner Mike's grandmother. Like all good Italian cooks, she insisted that the raw ingredients in any dish be ripe and flavorful. She never cheaped out and neither do we. When we started the Dinosaur Bar-B-Que, it was one of our original sides, and it has stayed on our menu ever since. It's best made in the morning, or at least several hours before serving.

The Veggies

1 ½ pounds ripe tomatoes
Pinch each of kosher salt and black pepper
Pinch of sugar
2 medium cucumbers
½ large red onion
30 small fresh basil leaves

The Dressing

½ cup extra virgin olive oil
¼ cup red wine vinegar
Black pepper
1 teaspoon kosher salt
4 cloves garlic, minced
1 teaspoon sugar
1 teaspoon dried oregano

Core the tomatoes and cut lengthwise into 6 to 8 wedges. Cut each wedge in half crosswise. Place the tomatoes in a big bowl and wake them up with a big pinch of salt, pepper, and sugar. Cut the ends off the cucumbers and use a vegetable peeler to make long stripes in the skin. Cut the cucumber in half lengthwise and then crosswise into ¼-inch slices. Add to the tomatoes. Peel the onion and cut lengthwise into slivers. Dump the onions in with the tomatoes and cucumbers and give everything a good tossing.

Clean and dry the basil leaves. Stack them on top of one another and then roll lengthwise into a tight cigar. Cut crosswise into thin strips and stir into the salad.

Throw together a batch of dressing. Whisk all the ingredients together in a small bowl. Pour over the tomatoes and cucumbers.

Marinate the salad at room temperature for several hours. Serve when you're ready, and then refrigerate the leftovers—if there are any. FEEDS 6

Whoever said money can't buy happiness doesn't know where to shop!!! —Dinosaur patron

Perfect Rice

Rice acts as a base for many a saucy dish, so you should never take it for granted. It's gotta be every bit as good as the food you serve it with. Rinsing the rice before cooking gets rid of the floury starch that clings to the grains and makes cooked rice sticky and lumpy, and adding some garlic boosts the flavor.

2 cups water
1 tablespoon olive oil
1 teaspoon kosher salt

2 cloves garlic, crushed
1 cup long-grain rice

Combine the water, olive oil, salt, and garlic in a saucepan. Turn up the heat and bring to a boil. Meanwhile, put the rice in a sieve and rinse under running water til the water loses its milky look and runs clear. Add the rice to the boiling water, cover the pan, reduce the heat to a simmer, and cook for 20 minutes. Fluff with a fork and cook a bit more if it seems too moist.
FEEDS 4

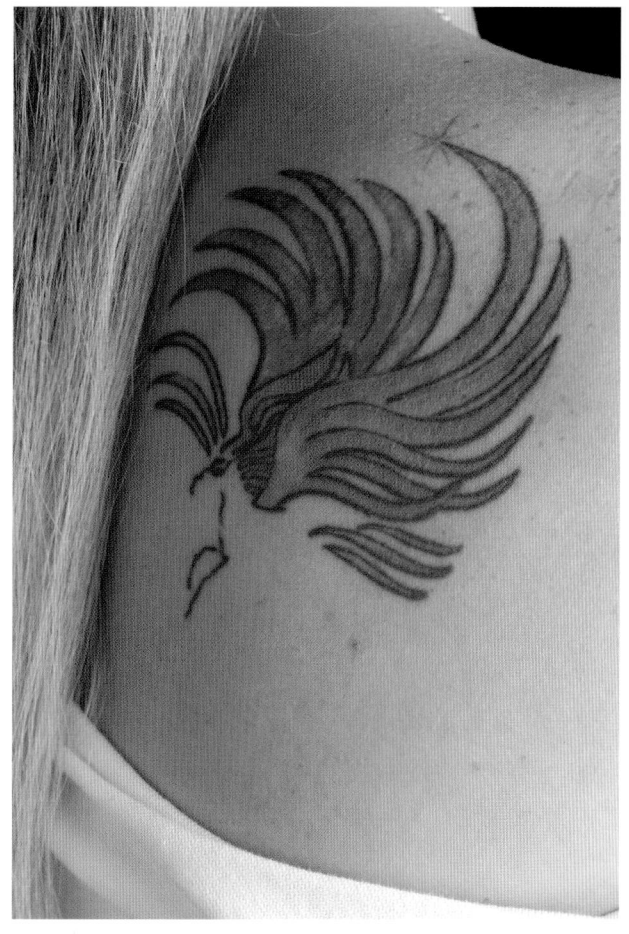

Dinosaur-Style Bar-B-Que Beans

These beans have a deep, broodin' flavor—sweet and spicy at the same time. We add crumbled hot Italian sausage to make 'em truly special.

2 tablespoons olive oil

½ large onion, chopped

¾ cup chopped green pepper

Pinch each of kosher salt and
    black pepper

3 large cloves garlic, chopped

8 ounces hot Italian sausage,
    removed from casing

2 cans (28 ounces each) baked beans,
    preferably Bush's

¾ cup Mutha Sauce (page 165)

1 tablespoon Creole mustard (preferably
    Zatarain's) or spicy brown mustard

1 tablespoon cider vinegar

1 teaspoon chili powder

½ teaspoon Creole Seasoning (page 167)

1 tablespoon molasses

Heat the olive oil in a large saucepan over medium-high heat. Add the onions and peppers and cook til soft, adding a pinch of salt and pepper. Toss in the garlic and cook for 1 minute more.

Crumble the sausage into the veggies and cook, chopping to break the meat into small pieces. Cook til the pink disappears. Drain off some of the bean liquid in each can so that it's at the same height as the beans; then mix the contents of both cans into the cooked veggies and sausage.

Turn the heat down to medium-low and add all the rest of the ingredients. Simmer for 5 minutes. Serve immediately, or cool and reheat before serving (lettin' the flavors blend a while never hurts). FEEDS 10 TO 12

Real men don't share half racks!
—Dinosaur lunch waitress

Black Beans & Rice

Serve up these deeply flavored Cuban-style beans with a pile of perfectly cooked white rice. Add a salad or some veggies and you've got the Dinosaur vegetarian platter.

The Beans

2 cups black beans
8 cups water
½ large onion, diced
½ green pepper, diced
2 large cloves garlic, chopped
1 bay leaf
1 tablespoon olive oil
1 ½ teaspoons kosher salt
Black pepper

The Sofrito

2 tablespoons vegetable oil
1 cup chopped onion
1 cup chopped green pepper
Pinch each of kosher salt and black pepper
3 large cloves garlic, chopped

The Finish

2 teaspoons ground cumin
1 tablespoon dried oregano
1 teaspoon kosher salt
1 tablespoon brown sugar
4 teaspoons red wine vinegar
Tabasco sauce
¼ cup dry sherry

The Accoutrement

Perfect Rice (page 117)

Sort through the beans and pull out any little stones or shriveled beans. Rinse the good beans and toss them into a large saucepan. Add 2 cups of the water, the onions, peppers, garlic, bay leaf, olive oil, salt, and pepper. Turn the heat up to high and bring to a boil. Cover the pan, cracking the lid a bit, and turn the heat down to low. Simmer for 2 to 2 ½ hours, adding the remaining water, 1 cup at a time, as it is absorbed by the beans. When they're done, the beans will give off a luscious black "gravy."

Grab a small saucepan for the sofrito (see note), and place it over medium heat. Add the oil. Toss in the onions and peppers, seasoning them with a pinch of salt and pepper. Once they're soft, add the garlic and cook another minute.

Dump the sofrito into the cooked beans. Pull out the bay leaf and finish the dish by stirring in the cumin, oregano, salt, brown sugar, vinegar, Tabasco, and sherry. Serve with a batch of Perfect Rice. FEEDS 4 TO 6

Note: In many Spanish-speaking countries a sofrito is used as a base for many sauces. It's usually made up of various chopped vegetables fried in oil.

Cajun Corn

This is our most popular "vegetable of the day." It shows up on the menu every Monday. It's damn simple and packed with flavor. When you can make it with fresh corn in season, it's even better.

¼ cup butter
1 tablespoon minced garlic
3 cups fresh or frozen corn kernels, cooked

5 teaspoons Creole Seasoning (page 167)
2 tablespoons chopped fresh Italian parsley

TOSS the butter in a skillet and melt it over medium-high heat. Stir in the garlic and cook just til soft but not brown. Dump in the corn and give it a stir. Add the Creole

Seasoning and cook for several minutes to warm up the corn and give it a bit of a toasty taste. Stir in the parsley. Scrape everything into a bowl and take it to the table. FEEDS 4

Bill Wharton, the Sauce Boss

Honey Hush Corn Bread

Any Southern cookin' conjures up corn bread. Ours is sweet and mellow and goes great with the tanginess of our bar-b-que.

1 ¼ cups yellow cornmeal
¼ cup sugar
¾ cup flour
1 ½ teaspoons baking powder
½ teaspoon baking soda
1 teaspoon kosher salt

1 cup buttermilk
2 eggs, slightly beaten
½ teaspoon vanilla
¼ cup melted butter
2 tablespoons honey

Set the oven at 350°. Grease an 8 by 8-inch baking pan with shortening. Pop the pan in the oven to heat while you're mixing up the corn bread.

Mix the cornmeal, sugar, flour, baking powder, baking soda, and salt in a bowl. Whisk together the buttermilk, eggs, vanilla, and melted butter in another bowl. Pour the wet ingredients into the dry and give them a good stir, just til everything is moistened.

Pull the hot greased pan from the oven and pour in the batter. Bake for 25 to 30 minutes, or til a toothpick inserted in the middle comes out clean. Take the corn bread out of the oven and brush the top with honey.

Cool for 10 minutes in the pan before cutting into squares. FEEDS 9

Variation: Cheddar-Jalapeño Honey Hush Corn Bread

Follow the recipe for Honey Hush Corn Bread, stirring 1 cup cubed extra-sharp Cheddar cheese and 2 medium jalapeño peppers, seeded and minced, into the batter right before pouring it into the pan. Bake for 30 to 35 minutes and glaze with honey in the same way.

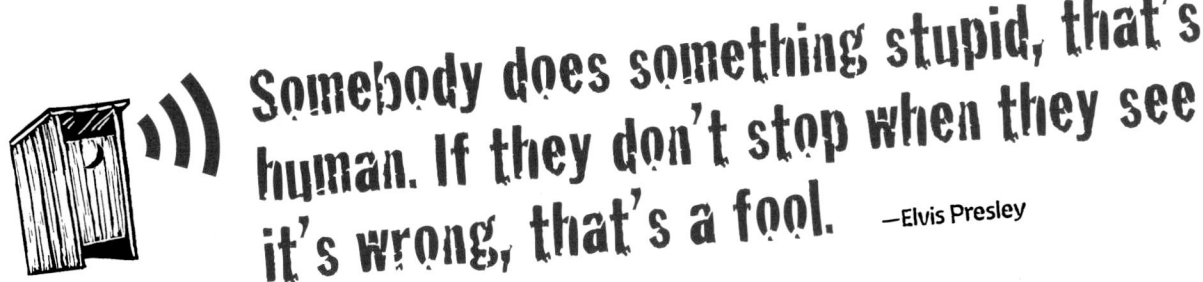

Somebody does something stupid, that's human. If they don't stop when they see it's wrong, that's a fool. —Elvis Presley

Fresh-Cut Fries

This recipe is so simple it's downright hard. We're talking about only three ingredients here—potatoes, oil, and salt. But you've got to pay close attention to those ingredients and their handling to come out with crispy, erect french fries. Make sure you read Fry Obsession (see below) before you start.

**Peanut oil to fill your deep-fryer
(about 1 gallon for a home fryer)**

**1 ½ large russet or all-purpose potatoes
per person
Kosher salt**

Fill a deep-fryer or a deep pan with oil. Heat to 325°. Wash and dry each potato well. Don't peel them. Cut the potatoes in half lengthwise and then into ½-inch fingers. Try to cut even pieces so you won't have any cooking issues later.

Blanch the fries in batches in hot oil. Don't crowd—a gallon fryer will hold 2 to 3 potatoes' worth of fries at a time. Cook for 7 to 8 minutes, til they give when you pinch them softly. Drain in a single layer on paper towels or brown paper bags, and let them cool down to room temperature.

Raise the temperature of the oil to 375°. Add the fries in batches (don't crowd them this time either) and fry again til golden and erect, another 7 to 8 minutes. Drain on paper towels or brown paper bags and season right away with salt. Serve as fast as you can—freshly cooked, hot, and crispy. FEEDS AS MANY AS YOU CARE TO FIX 'EM FOR

Fry Obsession

Every cook at the Dinosaur knows I'm a real pain in the balls when it comes to french fries. If their fries are flaccid I challenge their manhood. The fries have to be crisp and erect or they just don't cut it.

Fries have been my passion for as long as I can remember. But it wasn't til we started making them that I truly became obsessed. Between our two restaurants, we go through a mother lode of potatoes every week. So with that much at stake, I've become real fussy about the potatoes we use. That's because the secret to really great fries is locked into each and every potato. You won't know how age and type have affected its sugar and starch content til you fry it up.

Picking the right potato is key. For the most part, the russet potato is great, but at some times of the year we get better results from the all-purpose potato. Before we put in a big potato order, we'll have six or seven samples sent to the restaurant to test. When we find one that cooks up perfectly, we book it.

If you're lookin' to make great fries, why not test a couple of types of potatoes yourself to see which one performs best for you? Look for potatoes that are even in size and don't have any eyes or sprouts. Cut them evenly, and make sure they're nice and dry before you fry them. Peanut oil seems to be the best oil to use because it has a high smoking point and can be reused for several batches of fries on different days.

Garlic & Cheddar Grits

Most Yankees have a preconceived notion that they don't like grits. When we put them on the menu, lots of folks are resistant. It's a tough sell for the waitresses, but once they get customers to try them, they're hooked. Our flavor-boosted grits are rich and powerfully earthy. Serve them instead of mashed potatoes.

¼ cup butter
1 cup chopped onion
¾ cup chopped green pepper
1 medium jalapeño pepper, seeded
    and minced
Sprinkling plus 2 teaspoons kosher salt
Sprinkling plus 1 teaspoon black pepper

4 large cloves garlic, minced
4 cups whole milk
1 cup quick grits
1 cup shredded Cheddar cheese
¼ cup grated Pecorino Romano cheese
Tabasco sauce

Sling half of the butter into a saucepan and melt it over medium-high heat. Dump in the onions, peppers, and jalapeños. Season with a sprinkling of salt and pepper and cook til soft. Add the garlic and cook 1 minute more.

Pour in the milk, cover, and bring to a boil. (Watch it so it doesn't boil over.) Turn the heat down to medium-low and slowly stir in the grits. Cook, covered, for 5 minutes, stirring occasionally.

Pull the pan off the heat and hurl in the cheeses, 2 teaspoons salt, and 1 teaspoon pepper. Stir it around til the cheeses are melted and incorporated into the grits; then spice it all up with some Tabasco and fold in the remaining butter.

Spoon the grits up and serve pronto. Or, if serving later, butter a 9 by 13-inch baking pan and preheat the oven to 350°. Spoon in the grits and level with a spatula. Throw them into the oven and bake for 45 minutes. Cool and cut into geometric shapes for frying or grilling later.
FEEDS 6

God is love, love is blind. Therefore, God is Ray Charles. —Dinosaur patron, a true blueswoman

Bobby Green of A Cut Above

Mean Money Greens Revisited

Mean Money Greens are one of our special daily sides. We make 'em in the good old Southern manner—boiled with salt pork for hours til they melt in your mouth. Realizin' that this technique might not fit the time constraints of the modern cook, we've revisited this dish and can now give you an updated, healthier version that preserves most of the B vitamins found in collards and brings out their natural peppery flavor.

1 pound collard greens
¼ cup olive oil
1 red bell pepper, cut in 2-inch strips,
     ¼ inch wide
½ large onion, slivered
Sprinkling plus 1 teaspoon kosher salt

Sprinkling plus 1 teaspoon black pepper
4 large cloves garlic, minced
2 tablespoons red wine vinegar
Tabasco sauce
2 teaspoons honey

Slice off the stems from the collards right below the leaf, and discard the stems. Fill the sink with cold water and give the collard leaves a good soaking and washing to get rid of all the grit clinging to the folds of the leaves.

Drop the greens into a couple of inches of boiling salted water. Boil for 5 minutes. Drain and rinse in cold water. Drain again and chop coarsely.

Pour the olive oil into a large skillet. Toss in the peppers and onions, seasoning them with a sprinkling of salt and pepper. Once they're soft, toss in the garlic and cook 1 minute more. Dump in the greens and give them a stir. Add 1 teaspoon salt, 1 teaspoon pepper, the vinegar, Tabasco, and honey. Stir one more time and serve up a mess of healthy greens. FEEDS 4

Garlic & Ginger Green Beans

This recipe from our Rochester restaurant brings together the lively flavors of fresh garlic and ginger. It makes for a refreshin' salad that goes with all sorts of grilled and roasted meats and poultry.

The Beans

1 pound green beans
1 small red bell pepper, cut in thin strips
¼ cup slivered red onion
1 tablespoon minced garlic
1 tablespoon minced fresh ginger

The Dressing

¼ cup lime juice (about 1 big lime)
¼ cup red wine vinegar
1 teaspoon kosher salt
1 teaspoon Dijon mustard
2 teaspoons brown sugar
½ cup olive oil
½ cup Mutha Sauce (page 165)
1 rounded teaspoon grated orange zest

Cut the tips and stems off the green beans. Plunge them into a pot of boiling salted water and cook til tender-crisp. Drain and throw them into a bowl. Add the peppers, onions, garlic, and ginger.

Mix up the dressing by whisking the lime juice, vinegar, salt, mustard, and brown sugar in a bowl til the salt and sugar dissolve. Keep whisking and add the oil in a thin, steady stream. Splash in the Mutha Sauce and add the orange zest. Give it all a stir and pour over the veggies.

Mix well and let the beans marinate at room temperature for several hours before serving. FEEDS 4

Sautéed Green Beans
with Onions & Mushrooms

This is how my mother cooks green beans. They're so good and so simple that right from the start we made them our Tuesday vegetable of the day at the restaurant.

8 ounces mushrooms
1 pound green beans
1 clove garlic, crushed, plus 3 cloves
     garlic, minced
2 tablespoons olive oil

2 tablespoons butter
1 cup finely chopped onion
Kosher salt
Black pepper

Clean the mushrooms and slice ¼ inch thick through the cap and stem. Set aside. Cut the ends off the green beans and leave them long. Cook the beans in a pot of well-salted boiling water seasoned with the crushed garlic and 1 tablespoon of the olive oil til tender-crisp. Drain and set aside.

Sizzle the butter in a skillet set over medium-high heat. Add the onions with a pinch of salt and cook til soft. Toss in the minced garlic and cook 1 minute more.

Pour in the remaining tablespoon of olive oil and add the mushrooms. Turn the heat down to medium-low, cover the pan, and cook the mushrooms down til soft. Pile in the green beans, seasoning everything with salt and a generous amount of pepper. Stir it all up and serve while it's still pipin' hot. FEEDS 4

The Dinosaur Bar-B-Que... no black, no white, just blues.
—Dinosaur patron

Garlic Dill Pickles

I was eating at my favorite deli in the world—the Second Avenue Deli in New York City—when the pickle tray came out and inspiration hit. Why were we buyin' pickles when we could make our own to go with our sandwiches? So we came up with our own brand of Garlic Dill Pickles spiced up with slices of fresh jalapeño peppers. They're appetizing and guaranteed to get your taste buds tinglin'. Folks are always asking us to bottle 'em, but til we do you can make up your own batch. Keep 'em in a crock with a tight-fittin' lid in the fridge. They keep for weeks and weeks.

The Cukes

3 ¾ to 4 pounds pickling cucumbers
    (each 5 to 6 inches long)
¼ cup chopped garlic
2 jalapeño peppers, thinly sliced
    (seeds and all)
½ cup chopped fresh dill

The Brine

4 cups white vinegar
2 cups water
6 tablespoons kosher salt
½ cup sugar
5 heaping tablespoons pickling spice
2 tablespoons mustard seeds
2 tablespoons black peppercorns

Wash out a 3 ½-quart crock with hot, sudsy water. Rinse the crock really well and dry it.

Slice the cucumbers into ½-inch-thick rounds. Put them in a bowl with the garlic, jalapeños, and dill. Mix well and pile them in the crock.

Combine the remaining ingredients in a large saucepan and bring to a boil over high heat. Pull the pan off the stove and let the vinegar mixture cool for a couple of minutes. Then pour it over the cucumber slices, stirring everything up to distribute all the ingredients. Cool to room temperature. Cover the crock with its lid or with some plastic wrap and put it in the fridge. Let the pickles marinate for a week. Then you can start eatin' and eatin' and eatin'. They'll keep for weeks.   MAKES A MOTHER LODE

Personal magnetism is that indefinable something that enables us to get by without any ability. —Dinosaur patron

Zucchini & Eggplant Sauté

This is a good old Italian recipe that makes an appearance on our menu every once in a while. It's brimmin' with Old World flavors and looks damn good on the plate. It'll keep your main courses from gettin' boring.

The Veggies
1 ½ pounds eggplant
Kosher salt
2 medium zucchini
5 tablespoons olive oil
½ large onion, slivered
Black pepper

3 large cloves garlic, chopped
1 can (14 ½ ounces) diced tomatoes

The Garnish
½ cup freshly grated
   Parmigiano-Reggiano cheese
20 fresh basil leaves, chopped

Peel the eggplant and cut into 1-inch-thick rounds. Put them in a colander and sprinkle with salt. Let the eggplant sit and "weep" for 30 minutes to an hour. Then, if it's seedy, wipe off the seeds and squeeze the rounds firmly between paper towels to blot up all the moisture. Stack the rounds and cut them into quarters. Slice the zucchini in half lengthwise and then into ¾-inch slices.

Pour the oil into a skillet and heat over medium-high til hot and fragrant. Toss in the eggplant and fry for several minutes, til softened and tinged with brown. Grab a slotted spoon and gently remove the eggplant. Add more oil to the pan if it looks dry; then add the onions and season with salt and pepper. Cook for a couple of minutes, til they're soft, then throw in the zucchini. Turn up the heat and stir-fry til tender-crisp. Add the garlic and cook for 1 minute more.

Dump the tomatoes in, juice and all, and give the dish a good stir. Gently stir in the eggplant and taste to see how it's doing. Season with salt and pepper.

Scrape everything in the pan onto a good-looking platter and sprinkle with Parmigiano-Reggiano cheese. Toss the chopped basil on top of the finished dish and serve it up quick!
FEEDS 4 TO 6

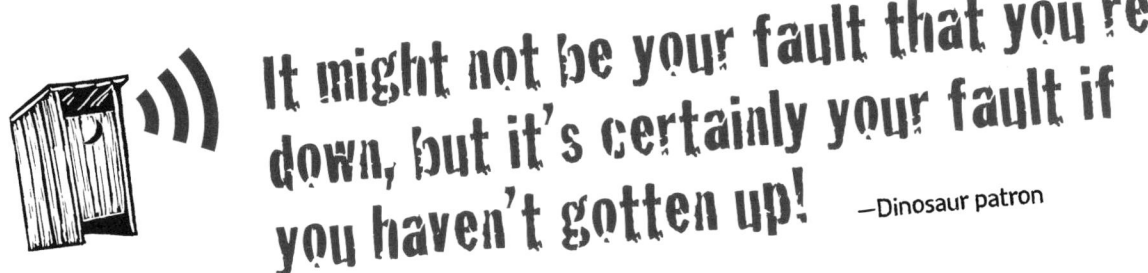

It might not be your fault that you're down, but it's certainly your fault if you haven't gotten up!
—Dinosaur patron

Soups and Leftovers

Bar-B-Que Layered Hash

If you were wonderin' what to do with all that leftover pulled pork or brisket you smoked, or if you have some nice roast turkey hangin' around, give this a try. It's our only breakfast item and it goes great with a couple of eggs on the side.

2 pounds all-purpose potatoes
⅓ plus ¼ cup vegetable oil
Kosher salt and black pepper
2 cups chopped onion
1 medium jalapeño pepper,
    seeded and minced

1 ½ pounds any type leftover meat or poultry,
    shredded or diced (about 6 cups)
1 ½ cups Mutha Sauce (page 165)
2 cups shredded Cheddar cheese
Creole Seasoning (page 167)
2 tablespoons sliced scallion

Preheat the oven to 425°. Set a kettle on the stove, fill it with salted water, and plop in the potatoes with their skins on. Get the pot boiling and cook the potatoes til very tender. Pull them out and peel them, then dice into ½-inch cubes and set aside.

Pour ⅓ cup oil into a heavy cast-iron skillet set over medium-high heat. Dump in the potatoes and spread them in an even layer covering the bottom of the pan. Season those spuds real well with salt and pepper. Cook for 8 to 10 minutes, til light golden brown. Peek under one section to check the browning before giving the whole thing a flip by putting a plate over the pan and flipping the potatoes onto the plate. Do this carefully, protecting your hands with potholder mitts. Scrape out any potatoes stuck to the pan. Then, if the pan looks dry, add a bit more oil and slide the potatoes back in, cooked side up. Cook for another 8 to 10 minutes, til golden and crispy.

Move the pan off the heat if you're not ready with the next layers.

Sling another pan onto the stove and turn the heat up to medium-high. Pour in ¼ cup oil and add the onions and jalapeños, seasoning them with salt and pepper. Once they're soft, add the leftover meat and Mutha Sauce and stir it all up.

Spread the meat mixture over the potatoes in an even layer, pressing it down with the back of a spatula. Throw on a layer of shredded cheese, and pop the pan into the hot oven for 15 minutes. Once the cheese is melted, pull the hash out and let it rest for 10 minutes to make for easier cutting. Sprinkle the top with Creole Seasoning and scallions. Cut into wedges and serve right from the pan.
FEEDS 4 TO 6

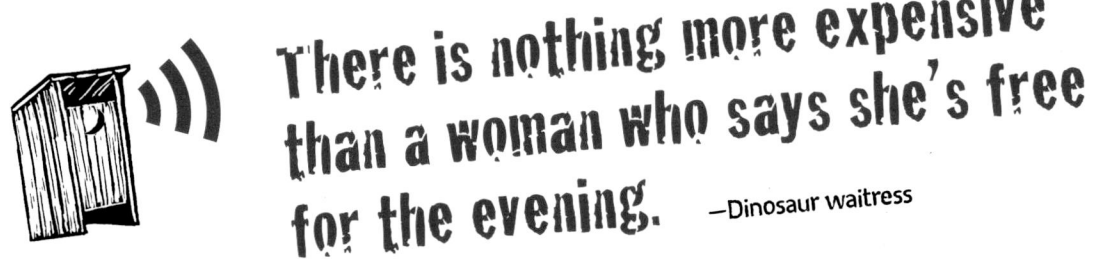

There is nothing more expensive than a woman who says she's free for the evening. —Dinosaur waitress

Chicken & Ham Jambalaya

Back in the early days of the Dinosaur Bar-B-Que, I made a pilgrimage to New Orleans, and it seemed natural to bring some of the wonders of the Big Easy back up north. The thing that really grabbed me was jambalaya, a dish with infinite possibilities. There's no one recipe for jambalaya because its whole reason for bein' is to let the cook get personal and real creative with the bits of meat or fish hangin' around in the fridge. You can give it your personal touch any way the spirit moves you. Try makin' it with other veggies, throwin' in some shellfish, messin' with the seasoning—this is your chance to be a link in the evolution of one truly great leftover dish.

½ cup vegetable oil
1 ½ cups chopped onion
1 ¼ cups chopped green pepper
1 cup chopped celery
1 medium jalapeño pepper,
    seeded and minced
Kosher salt and black pepper
2 tablespoons minced garlic
1 ½ pounds boneless, skinless chicken thighs,
    cut in 2-inch cubes
1 pound baked ham, cut in 1-inch cubes

2 cups chicken broth or stock (to make your
    own, see page 168)
1 cup crushed tomatoes
½ cup Mutha Sauce (page 165)
1 bay leaf
1 ¾ cups parboiled long-grain rice
    (preferably Uncle Ben's)
Tabasco sauce
1 teaspoon dried thyme
¼ teaspoon cayenne pepper
½ cup sliced scallion

Pour the oil into a large Dutch oven and set it over medium-high heat. Once it's hot, add the onions, green peppers, celery, and jalapeños. Season with salt and pepper and cook til soft and tinged with brown. Toss in the garlic and cook for 1 minute more; then add the chicken. Cook for about 4 minutes, turning the pieces and mixing them with the veggies.

Stir in the ham and pour in the broth, tomatoes, and Mutha Sauce. Now drop in the bay leaf and dump in the rice. Give everything a stir, and spice it up with some Tabasco. Bring to a boil, then cover the pot and turn down the heat to a low simmer. Cook for 25 minutes without stirring.

Uncover and fish out the bay leaf. Mix everything well. Season with lots of freshly ground black pepper, and add the thyme, cayenne, and scallions. Then spoon it up.
FEEDS 4 GENEROUSLY AS A MAIN COURSE OR 8 AS AN APPETIZER

Note: Here's a double leftover idea. Take leftover jambalaya and stuff it into hollowed-out peppers or tomatoes. Bake at 350° til the veggie containers are soft, 30 minutes for tomatoes or 45 minutes for peppers. Serve with some Mutha Sauce ladled over the top.

Texas Red Chili

Texans like meat, and in Texas, chili is all about meat and spices. We make ours with chunks of sirloin and season it with a blend of ancho chiles, which lend an earthy, sweet, raisin flavor, and pasilla chiles, which give a spicy, deep taste. Our Texas Red Chili is a "wanderin' special" on our menu, showin' up every now and then. During deer season in November, we may even make it with venison.

3 ½ to 4 pounds beef sirloin or stew meat
Kosher salt
Coarsely ground black pepper
1 tablespoon corn oil
¼ pound bacon, diced
3 cups chopped onion
2 cups chopped green pepper
2 medium jalapeño peppers, seeded
    and minced
2 heaping tablespoons chopped garlic
4 cups beef broth or stock (to make your own,
    see page 169)
1 can (28 ounces) crushed tomatoes

2 bay leaves
1 cinnamon stick (2 ½ to 3 inches long)
2 tablespoons ground ancho chile (see note)
1 tablespoon ground pasilla chile (see note)
2 teaspoons ground cumin
1 ½ tablespoons brown sugar
1 tablespoon dried oregano
Juice of ½ lime
2 tablespoons chopped fresh cilantro

The Garnish
Shredded Cheddar cheese
Chopped red onions

Trim away the fat and membrane from the meat and cut into 1-inch cubes. Season the meat with 1 tablespoon each of salt and pepper and set aside.

Heat the oil in a large Dutch oven. Toss in the bacon and cook over medium-high heat til brown and crispy. Scoop out the bacon and drain on some paper towels. (The bacon is only for flavoring the oil in the pot, so feel free to eat up all the crispy bits while you cook.) Keep the bacon fat in the pan and add the beef in batches. Cook each batch for about 3 minutes, stirring the pieces around til browned. Scoop each batch out into a bowl when it's done.

Toss the onions, green peppers, and jalapeños into the pot and stir them around in the pan juices, scraping up all the tasty brown bits clinging to the bottom and sides of the pot. Season the veggies with a generous pinch of salt and pepper, and cook til soft. Add the garlic and cook for 1 minute more. Dump all the meat and any accumulated meat juices into the veggies. Add the broth, tomatoes, bay leaves, cinnamon stick, chiles,

cumin, and brown sugar and give everything a good stir. Cover the pan and bring to a boil; then crack the lid, turn down the heat to low, and simmer for 1 ½ to 2 hours, or til the beef is nice and tender but still holds its shape.

Finish the chili by adding the oregano, lime juice, and cilantro. Fish out the cinnamon stick and the bay leaves, then check the seasonings and add a bit more salt and pepper if you like. Ladle the chili out into bowls and top with some shredded Cheddar cheese and chopped red onions. It's lip-tinglin' good. FEEDS 8 TO 12

Note: Ancho and pasilla chiles can most commonly be found whole and dried (locally in Syracuse at the Hot Shoppe in Armory Square; see Resources, page 174). If you wind up with whole dried chiles, you'll need to crisp them up a bit before grinding them yourself. So preheat the oven to 300° and toast the chiles for 3 to 5 minutes, til crisp and dry. Slit the sides and get the seeds out. Break the chiles into pieces and grind in a spice mill or coffee grinder.

Chicken & Sausage Gumbo

Here's another good old Louisiana dish we transported north for our menu. We thought its distinctive spicy, earthy taste was just what our customers were cravin'. Our gumbo is thick like a good hearty stew, and although we've personalized it, we've still kept it related to all other gumbos by thickening it with Brown Roux (page 139). The flour toasted in oil makes a dusky mix that binds all the veggies, meats, and seasonings into a veritable swamp of broodin' flavors.

The Gumbo

¼ cup vegetable oil

1 ½ pounds boneless, skinless chicken thighs, cut into 2-inch chunks

1 pound smoked sausage (andouille, chorizo, or kielbasa), sliced

5 ¼ cups chicken broth or stock (to make your own, see page 168)

1 ½ cups chopped onion

¾ cup chopped celery

1 cup chopped green pepper

1 jalapeño pepper, seeded and minced

Pinch each of kosher salt and black pepper

2 tablespoons minced garlic

1 ½ cups Brown Roux (page 139)

2 bay leaves

2 teaspoons dried thyme

Tabasco sauce

¼ cup chopped fresh Italian parsley

The Accoutrement

8 cups Perfect Rice
    (page 117—make a double recipe)

Heat up the oil in a heavy-bottomed soup kettle over medium-high heat til hot but not smoking. Add the chicken in batches so you're not crowding the pieces. Cook, turning pieces often, til they're lightly browned, 4 to 5 minutes. As the pieces get done, toss them into a bowl. Add the sausage slices to the same pot and cook long enough to render out the fat. Pluck the sausage out of the pot and drain on paper towels.

Pour off all but ¼ cup of fat from the pot. Swish the pot with ¼ cup of the broth, scraping in all the tasty bits. Put the pot back on the stove and throw in the onions, celery, green peppers, and jalapeños, seasoning them with a pinch of salt and pepper. Cook til soft over medium-high and then add the garlic and cook for 1 minute more. Add the Brown Roux and give everything a good stir. Whisk in the remaining 5 cups of broth. Dump in the chicken along with any accumulated juices (no sausage yet), and throw in the bay leaves.

Cover the pan and bring the contents to a boil. Turn down the heat to a simmer and cook for about 1 hour. Every now and then, skim the oil that comes to the surface and give the gumbo a stir. Once the gumbo gets a nice velvety look, toss the sausage back in and season with thyme and a generous amount of Tabasco. Pull out the bay leaves, check the seasonings, and sprinkle with parsley.

Spoon some Perfect Rice into a bunch of bowls. Ladle the gumbo over it and bring it to the table. FEEDS 6 TO 8

Brown Roux

You just can't make gumbo without a good brown roux. It's the heart and soul of any self-respectin' gumbo. Our version cooks in 20 minutes and you have to give it your full attention. There's a fine line between brown roux and burnt roux.

1 cup vegetable oil

1 cup flour

Pour the oil into a saucepan. Slide it over medium heat and get the oil nice and hot. Whisk in the flour. Cook, whisking constantly—it will be a bit grainy at first. Soon the flour will start turning color. This will deepen with every passing minute. You're aiming to get a nice chocolate brown color and a rich, nutty, toasted smell. So open up your senses and keep whisking. Once the roux reaches the perfect color and smell, pull the pan off the heat and keep whisking as it cools down a bit. It will get thinner and smoother. Use the roux right away or pour it into a plastic container and let it cool down completely. Refrigerate til you need it.
MAKES 1½ CUPS

Soulful Stew

Here's a stew that comes and goes on our menu, rotating with a couple of other meat stews. It's lighter than the others and is simmered with ten different vegetables. It's healthy food for your meat-lovin' soul.

10 ounces fresh spinach

2 pounds boneless, skinless chicken thighs
    or breasts

½ cup flour

Kosher salt and black pepper

½ cup olive oil

2 cups chopped onion

1 ¼ cups chopped green pepper

1 cup chopped celery

1 jalapeño pepper, seeded and minced

1 pound baked ham, diced

4 to 6 cloves garlic, minced

1 bay leaf

1 cup chicken broth or stock (to make your
    own, see page 168)

1 can (14 ½ ounces) diced tomatoes

1 cup Mutha Sauce (page 165)

1 tablespoon Worcestershire sauce

2 cups sliced carrots

1 can (15 ounces) black-eyed peas, drained

1 can (15 ounces) corn kernels, drained

1 teaspoon ground cumin

1 teaspoon dried thyme

1 tablespoon dried oregano

Tabasco sauce

Strip any large, tough stems from the spinach and give it a good washing. Dry the leaves in a salad spinner or pat dry. Stack 10 leaves on top of one another and roll them up like a cigar. Slice into wide ribbons. Continue til all the leaves are sliced; set aside.

Cut the chicken into 1 by ¾-inch strips. Season the flour with salt and pepper, and toss the chicken in it. Set a large Dutch oven on the stove and heat 6 tablespoons of the olive oil over medium-high. Add the chicken in batches and brown lightly. As the chicken gets done, scoop it out of the pot into a bowl. Set aside.

Add the remaining 2 tablespoons of oil to the pot if it looks dry, and toss in the onions, green peppers, celery, and jalapeños, seasoning them with a pinch of salt and pepper. Stir in the ham and garlic and cook for

2 minutes more. Dump the chicken back in, along with its juices. Add the bay leaf, broth, tomatoes, Mutha Sauce, Worcestershire, and carrots. Cover the pot and bring everything to a boil; then crack the lid, turn down the heat to low, and simmer til the carrots are soft, 15 to 20 minutes.

Uncover the pot and throw in the black-eyed peas, corn, and spinach. Season the stew with the cumin, thyme, and oregano, and let everything simmer for another 15 minutes to blend the flavors. Take out the bay leaf and taste the stew to see if it needs some salt and pepper; then spice everything up with Tabasco.

Serve the stew steamin' hot in great big soup bowls.
FEEDS 10 TO 12

Split Pea Soup

Now this is real comfort food. It makes me feel like I'm doing something good for myself every time I eat it. Delicious and healthy—what more do you want?

2 tablespoons butter

2 tablespoons olive oil

2 cups finely diced onion

1 cup finely diced celery

Kosher salt and black pepper

2 tablespoons chopped garlic

9 cups chicken broth or stock (to make your own, see page 168)

2 cups split peas

1 bay leaf

2 cups diced ham

¾ cup shredded carrot

2 cups frozen peas

1 scant teaspoon dried thyme

Tabasco sauce

Toss the butter into a soup kettle and add the olive oil. Melt them together over medium-high heat. Then add the onions and celery, seasoning with a pinch of salt and pepper. Cook til the veggies are soft; then add the garlic and cook for 1 minute more. Douse with the broth, dump in the split peas, and drop in the bay leaf. Cover and bring the broth to a boil; then crack the lid and turn down the heat to low. Simmer 45 minutes, or til the peas start to soften. With the back of a slotted spoon, press down on the peas in the pot to crush them a bit. Simmer for another 15 to 30 minutes, til the peas are nice and soft.

Stir in the ham, carrots, and frozen peas. Season the soup with thyme, freshly ground black pepper, and some more salt if you think it needs it. Now perk everything up with Tabasco, and simmer gently 5 minutes more. Fish out the bay leaf, pour the soup into bowls, and serve.
FEEDS 8

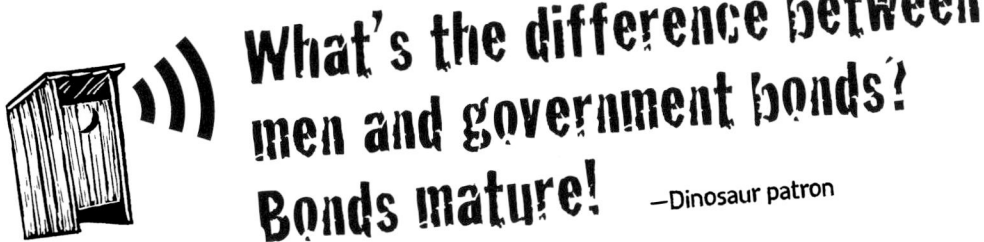

What's the difference between men and government bonds? Bonds mature! —Dinosaur patron

Corn & Potato Chowder

This has been the Dinosaur's Wednesday soup special for as long as I can remember. It's a good, hearty soup that's perfect for places like Syracuse and Rochester, New York, that are blessed with six months of winter a year—not that folks stop eating Corn & Potato Chowder in the summer. Made with fresh corn, just picked and cut from the cob, this soup takes on a real summer attitude. Best of all, you can make it in less than half an hour any time of the year.

1 tablespoon butter ~~or~~ omit
¼ pound bacon, diced
1 cup chopped onion
¾ cup chopped green pepper
2 med celery stalks, Diced
Kosher salt and black pepper
1 tablespoon minced garlic
2 tablespoons flour
4 cups chicken broth or stock
   (to make your own, see page 168)

4 cups peeled, finely diced all-purpose potato
1 ½ cups shredded carrot
2 cups fresh or frozen corn kernels
1 cup half-and-half
½ teaspoon dried thyme
Pinch of cayenne pepper
2 tablespoons chopped fresh Italian parsley

Sling the butter into a soup kettle and melt over medium-high heat. Add the bacon and cook til crisp. Scoop out the bacon and drain on paper towels. Save for later—don't nibble too much.

Pour

off all but ¼ cup of *2T* fat from the pot. Toss in the onions and peppers, seasoning them with a pinch of salt and pepper. Cook til soft and then throw in the garlic, cooking it all for 1 minute more. Sprinkle on the flour and mix into the veggies. Dump in the broth and potatoes. Cover the pot and bring to a boil; then lower the heat and simmer for 10 to 12 minutes, or til the potatoes are tender. Add the shredded carrots and corn. Cover and simmer everything 5 to 6 minutes longer to blend the flavors.

Stir in the half-and-half. Season with the thyme, cayenne, some more salt, and lots of freshly ground black pepper to taste. Sprinkle with parsley and the bacon bits you've been saving. Give it one last stir, and ladle it up piping hot.   FEEDS 6 TO 8

Tomato & Roasted Garlic Soup

A few years back, we were closed on Sunday. People kept turnin' up anyway, so we gave in and opened with a limited menu. We created this soup just for that day. It has a good Sunday vibe.

¼ cup butter

2 tablespoons olive oil

1 ¼ cups chopped onion

1 cup chopped green pepper

Pinch each kosher salt and black pepper

1 ½ tablespoons minced garlic

2 tablespoons flour

4 cups chicken broth or stock
    (to make your own, see page 168)

1 bulb Roasted Garlic (page 170)

1 can (28 ounces) crushed tomatoes

1 bay leaf

1 cup heavy cream

½ cup freshly grated
    Parmigiano-Reggiano cheese

Tabasco sauce

2 tablespoons freshly squeezed lemon juice

20 fresh basil leaves, chopped

Drop 2 tablespoons of the butter into a soup kettle along with the olive oil. Melt them together over medium-high heat and add the onions and peppers; season with a pinch of salt and pepper. Once they're soft, toss in the minced garlic and cook for 1 minute more. Sprinkle on the flour and stir it in well; then pour in the broth and mix.

Squeeze the roasted garlic cloves out of their skins into a small bowl and mash to a paste. Stir the paste into the soup and bring to a boil. Add the tomatoes and the bay leaf. Bring to a boil again, cover the pot, and drop the heat back down to low. Simmer for 15 minutes, til heated through. Remove the bay leaf and pour in the cream. Add the Parmigiano-Reggiano and zip up the taste with a generous amount of Tabasco. Now stir in the lemon juice, the remaining 2 tablespoons of butter, and half of the chopped basil.

Ladle the soup into bowls and sprinkle the rest of the basil on top. FEEDS 6 TO 8

Never play leapfrog with a unicorn.
—Ancient Chinese proverb

Dirty Rice

This is the ultimate "anything goes" dish. All you need is some sausage and any kind of raw or cooked meat you might have on hand. We use a tasty mix of sausage, chicken, pulled pork, and ham. The only thing you can't skip are the chicken livers. That's what makes Dirty Rice dirty and gives it its deep, rich flavor. We've been servin' it every Wednesday as a featured side, and we've found that Central New Yorkers really appreciate this frugal New Orleans specialty. It's also good as a stuffing for Cornish hens, pork chops, or turkey.

⅓ cup olive oil

2 cups chopped onion

1 cup chopped green pepper

1 or 2 jalapeño peppers, seeded and minced

Kosher salt and black pepper

2 tablespoons minced garlic

½ pound boneless, skinless chicken thighs, cut in 2-inch cubes

1 pound bulk sweet Italian sausage

¼ pound leftover ham, cut in strips or cubes (about 1 cup)

¼ pound leftover meat of any kind, shredded or diced (about 1 cup)

½ pound chicken livers, puréed in a food processor

3 cups chicken broth or stock (to make your own, see page 168)

¼ teaspoon cayenne pepper

1 teaspoon ground cumin

1 teaspoon dried oregano

1 bay leaf

1 ½ cups parboiled long-grain rice (preferably Uncle Ben's)

Set a Dutch oven on the burner. Pour in the oil and get it nice and hot over medium-high heat. Toss in the onions, green peppers, and jalapeños. Season with salt and pepper. Cook til tinged with brown; then add the garlic and cook 1 minute more. Toss in the cubed chicken and cook, stirring, til the pieces are coated with the veggies. Crumble in the sausage and keep cooking and stirring til it loses its pink color. Toss in the remaining meats and the liver purée. Douse the meats with the broth and add the cayenne, cumin, oregano, and bay leaf. Stir in the rice and bring it all to a boil. Cover and turn the heat down low. Cook for 20 minutes without stirring. Pull the pot off the stove and remove the bay leaf. Now give it a stir and it's ready to serve. FEEDS 4 AS A MAIN COURSE OR 8 AS A SIDE DISH OR STUFFING PORTION

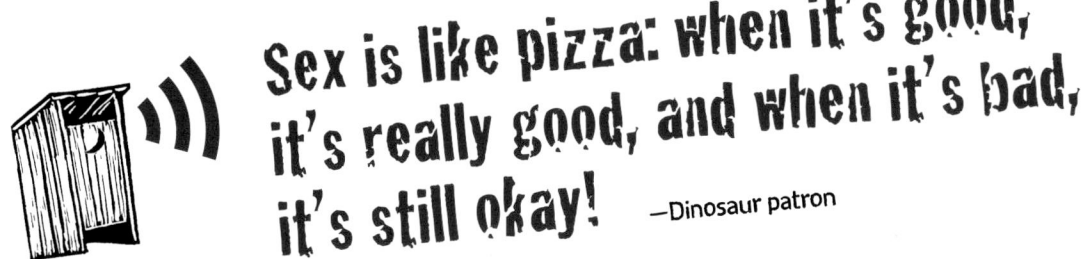

Sex is like pizza: when it's good, it's really good, and when it's bad, it's still okay! —Dinosaur patron

Desserts

Peanut Butter Pie

Pie doesn't get any easier than this. The chocolate cookie crust is pressed into the pan, and the filling needs no baking. It's the perfect dessert to whip up after you've invested all those hours smokin' your pork butt.

The Crust
20 Oreo sandwich cookies
3 tablespoons butter, melted

The Filling
1 cup heavy cream
1 tablespoon vanilla

8 ounces cream cheese, softened (preferably Philadelphia)
1 ¼ cups smooth peanut butter
1 cup confectioners' sugar

The Garnish
½ cup chopped peanuts

Throw the crust together. Crumble the cookies into the workbowl of a food processor, and process to crumbs. This will give you about 2 cups. Put them in a bowl and mix in the melted butter. Press the crumbs evenly over the bottom and up the sides of a 9-inch pie pan. Chill while making the filling.

Put the cream, vanilla, cream cheese, peanut butter, and confectioners' sugar in a mixer bowl. Mix on low for 1 minute, til blended, then gradually increase the speed to high. Whip til light and fluffy, about 1 more minute.

Spoon the filling into the chilled pie shell. Even off the top and sprinkle with peanuts. Pop into the fridge and let it chill til set, about 4 hours. Serve chilled and cut into wedges. Don't leave it out at room temperature for too long because it will soften too much. FEEDS 6 TO 8

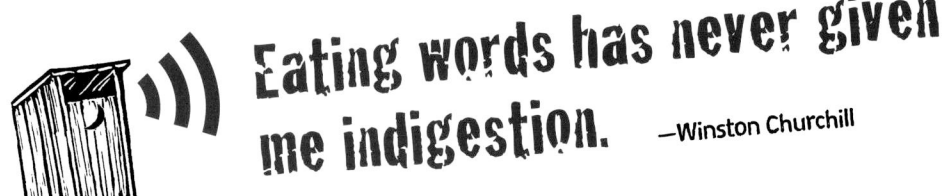

Eating words has never given me indigestion. —Winston Churchill

Chocolate Icebox Pie

Dino waitresses love this pie. It's rich chocolate pudding in a chocolate cookie crumb pie shell, and it's guaranteed to satisfy all your chocolate cravings.

The Crust
20 Oreo sandwich cookies
3 tablespoons butter, melted

The Filling
1 cup sugar
3 tablespoons cornstarch
⅓ cup flour
¼ teaspoon kosher salt

⅛ teaspoon ground cinnamon
1 cup chocolate chips
3 cups milk
3 large egg yolks
1 tablespoon vanilla

The Garnish
Sweetened whipped cream

Start with the crust. Crumble the cookies into the workbowl of a food processor and process to crumbs. This will give you about 2 cups. Put them in a bowl and mix in the melted butter. Press the crumbs evenly over the bottom and up the sides of a 9-inch pie pan. Chill.

Get busy making the filling. Sift the sugar, cornstarch, flour, salt, and cinnamon together into a bowl and set aside.

Combine the chocolate chips and milk in a saucepan and set it over medium heat, stirring constantly. As soon as the chips are melted, pull the pan off the heat and pour half of the chocolate mixture into the dry ingredients. Mix well.

Whisk the yolks and vanilla together in a bowl and pour into the remaining chocolate in the saucepan. Stir it around and then add the chocolate and dry ingredient mixture. Set the saucepan back over medium heat and whisk like crazy. Once the mixture starts to thicken, keep whisking and cooking for 2 minutes. Pour the chocolate filling into a bowl to cool for 10 minutes; then dump it into the pie shell and level the top. Chill for several hours in the fridge. Cut into wedges and serve slathered with whipped cream. FEEDS 6 TO 8

Dr Pepper Texas Chocolate Cake

The magic ingredient in this outrageous two-layer dark chocolate cake is Dr Pepper, one of America's oldest soft drinks. Dr Pepper was first made and sold in 1885 at Morrison's Old Corner Drug Store in Waco, Texas. Just like the state it comes from, this cake is big and impressive. The soft drink's carbonation gives the layers exceptional rising power, and its special blend of flavorings makes lickin' the beaters especially appealing.

The Cake

2 cups sifted flour

1 cup sugar

1 cup dark brown sugar

1 cup unsweetened cocoa powder

1 ½ teaspoons baking soda

1 cup Dr Pepper

½ cup chocolate chips

2 large eggs

1 cup buttermilk

1 cup vegetable oil

1 ½ teaspoons vanilla

The Frosting

¾ cup butter-flavored
    vegetable shortening

6 tablespoons unsalted butter, softened

4 cups sifted confectioners' sugar

¼ cup unsweetened cocoa powder

¼ cup Dr Pepper

1 ½ teaspoons vanilla

Get the oven heating to 350°. Grease and flour two 9-inch-round cake pans, tapping out any extra flour.

Sift together the flour, sugar, brown sugar, cocoa, and baking soda into a bowl and set aside. Pour the Dr Pepper into a saucepan and add the chocolate chips. Heat on low, stirring often, til the chips are just melted. Pull off the heat and set aside.

Combine the eggs, buttermilk, oil, and vanilla in a mixer bowl and mix on medium speed til combined, about 2 minutes. With the mixer running, slowly pour in the Dr Pepper-chocolate mixture and continue beating til combined, about 1 minute.

Drop the mixer speed back to low and gradually add the dry ingredients. Pop the speed back up to medium and beat 2 minutes more. Divide the batter between the 2 pans.

Bake 30 to 35 minutes, or til a toothpick poked into the center comes out clean. Cool the layers in the pans for 10 minutes, then run a knife around the edges and flip the pans over onto a cooling rack. Gently lift off the pans and let the cake layers cool completely.

Whip up the frosting. First drop the shortening and butter into a mixer bowl and beat til soft and fluffy. Add the confectioners' sugar and cocoa and continue mixing til combined. Stir together the Dr Pepper and vanilla and very slowly pour it into the frosting, beating with the mixer on high speed to thin it down a bit. Continue beating til light and fluffy, about 1 minute.

Set 1 layer, top down, on a good-looking plate. Smear on 1 cup of the frosting. Grab the other layer and slap it on top of the frosted one. Spread the rest of the frosting all over the top and sides of the cake, making attractive swirls. Serve, and accept the compliments. FEEDS 12

Coconut Bread Pudding
with Rum Cream Sauce

There are thousands of recipes for bread pudding because it's a classic for usin' up leftovers. I think some of the best recipes come from New Orleans, where home cooks and restaurant chefs alike treat this humble dish with great respect. That's where I got the inspiration for ours, which is pillow soft when warm and burstin' with plump raisins and chewy bits of coconut.

The Pudding

1 pound day-old Italian- or French-style bread

4 cups (1 quart) whole milk

2 teaspoons vanilla

2 cups sugar

½ teaspoon ground cinnamon

¼ teaspoon ground nutmeg

4 large eggs

2 large egg yolks

½ cup raisins

1 cup flaked coconut

¼ cup butter, softened

2 tablespoons confectioners' sugar

The Sauce

1 cup heavy cream

1 cup confectioners' sugar

½ cup butter, cut in 8 pieces

2 tablespoons rum

Set the dial to 325° and get the oven heating. Cut the crusts off the bread (save them for bread crumbs), and then cut the rest into 1-inch cubes, collecting about 8 cups. If the bread isn't day old, pop it into the heating oven for 5 to 10 minutes to dry it out a bit.

Whisk together the milk, vanilla, sugar, cinnamon, nutmeg, eggs, and yolks in a large bowl. Stir in the raisins, coconut, and bread cubes. Soak for 30 minutes.

Mix 2 tablespoons of the softened butter with the confectioners' sugar and smear it over the bottom and sides of a 9 by 13-inch pan. Pour in the bread-and-egg mixture. Melt the remaining 2 tablespoons of softened butter and drizzle it over the top. Pop the pan into the oven and bake for 50 to 60 minutes, or til set in the middle and puffed and brown around the edges.

Make the sauce while the pudding is baking. Combine the cream, confectioners' sugar, and butter in a saucepan. Set it over medium-high heat and bring to a boil. Keep your eye on it so it doesn't boil over. Whisk constantly. Turn the heat to low and simmer for 3 minutes; then stir in the rum. Keep warm. (Makes 1 ¾ cups of sauce.)

Pull the pan out of the oven when the bread pudding is done, and let it set for 10 minutes. Cut into squares and serve warm or at room temperature. Douse each serving with some warm sauce. FEEDS 12

Rice Pudding

I used to think I made a pretty good rice pudding. Then I went down to Miami and tasted the Cuban version, and I sent myself back to the stove. Now ours is modeled after the best ones I tasted down there. It's perfumed with a bit of lime peel and has a creamy texture and a smooth taste spiked with rum.

The Pudding

4 cups (1 quart) half-and-half
1 cinnamon stick (3 inches long)
Peel from ¼ lime (all white
    pith removed)
½ cup sugar
Pinch of kosher salt
¾ cup parboiled long-grain rice
    (preferably Uncle Ben's)

¾ cup heavy cream
2 egg yolks, lightly beaten
2 teaspoons vanilla
2 tablespoons brown sugar
2 tablespoons dark rum

The Garnish

Fresh mango cubes and
    whipped cream (optional)

Mix up the half-and-half, cinnamon stick, lime peel, sugar, and salt in a large saucepan. Slide it onto a burner and bring the mixture up to a simmer on medium-high heat. Dump in the rice and turn the heat down to low. Cook gently, stirring every now and then, for 35 to 40 minutes, or til the rice grains are just tender. Pull the pan off the heat.

Grab a bowl and whisk together the cream, yolks, vanilla, brown sugar, and rum. Fold the mixture into the cooked rice and put the pan back on medium heat for a few more minutes, stirring til the mixture just begins to thicken. Take it off the heat, fish out the cinnamon stick and the lime peel, and scrape the pudding into a bowl. Serve warm or cold just as it is, or dress the pudding up a bit with some fresh mango cubes and whipped cream.   FEEDS 4 TO 6

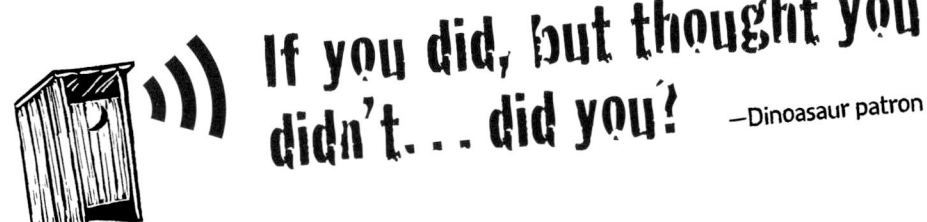

If you did, but thought you didn't. . . did you?   —Dinoasaur patron

Key Lime Pie

Key limes from Florida make their way up north to our markets only every once in awhile.
So we use regular limes. The real key is not to overbake the filling so it stays creamy.

The Crust
About 18 graham crackers
¼ cup sugar
½ teaspoon ground cinnamon
5 tablespoons butter, melted

The Filling
4 extra-large egg yolks,
lightly beaten

1 can (14 ounces) sweetened
condensed milk
1 ½ teaspoons grated lime zest
½ cup lime juice (from 3 or 4 limes)

The Garnish
Sweetened whipped cream

Preheat the oven to 350° and get busy making the pie crust. Break the graham crackers into the workbowl of a food processor and process to crumbs. You should have 1 ¼ cups. Mix the crumbs, sugar, and cinnamon together in a bowl. Pour on the butter and mix til the crumbs are evenly moistened. Press the crumbs into the bottom and up the sides of an 8-inch pie pan. Set aside.

Make the filling by whisking together the yolks, condensed milk, zest, and juice in a bowl. Pour the mixture into the crumb crust and bake for 20 to 25 minutes, or til the edges and the center are just set.

Pull the pie out of the oven and cool to room temperature; then chill it in the fridge. Slice into wedges and serve with a dollop of sweetened whipped cream.
FEEDS 6 TO 8

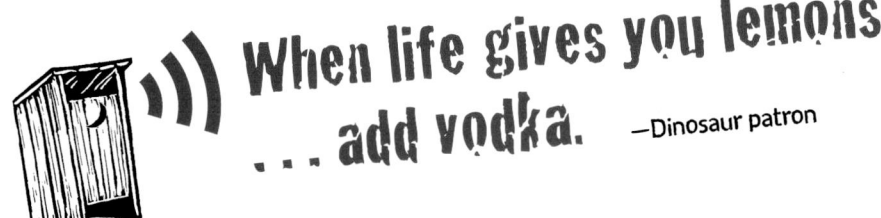
When life gives you lemons
. . . add vodka. —Dinosaur patron

Sweet Potato Pecan Pie

We've rolled two New Orleans classic pies into one to make a rich, deep, and satisfying dessert. It's a real restaurant favorite that has been known to make visitors from the South go wild.

The Crust
Dough for One-Crust Pie (page 172)

The Filling
2 cups cooked, mashed sweet potato
   (about 1 pound potatoes)
¾ cup sugar
2 large eggs, lightly beaten
½ teaspoon kosher salt
¼ teaspoon ground nutmeg
½ teaspoon ground cinnamon
¼ teaspoon ground allspice
½ teaspoon vanilla
⅔ cup sweetened condensed milk

The Topping
1 cup coarsely chopped pecans
2 large eggs, beaten
2 tablespoons butter, softened
2 teaspoons vanilla
½ cup sugar
½ cup dark corn syrup
Pinch of kosher salt
⅛ teaspoon ground cinnamon

The Garnish
Sweetened whipped cream

Preheat the oven to 325°. Pick out a 9 by 1¼-inch pie pan. This is a bit deeper than normal in order to hold everything. Roll out the pie crust, fit it into the pie pan as directed, and chill it in the freezer til you're ready for it.

Grab a big bowl and dump all the ingredients for the filling into it. Mix well and set the mixture aside.

Now take another bowl and throw in all the ingredients for the topping into it. Stir together and set aside.

Pull the pie shell out of the freezer and spoon in the filling. Smooth and even the surface. Then pour the topping over it. Pop the pie into the oven and bake for 1½ hours, or til the crust is golden and the filling is set. Cool the pie on a rack. Serve slices of pie at room temperature with a nice plop of sweetened whipped cream. FEEDS 8

Nancy's Own
Apple-Cranberry Crisp

This one's from my co-author. Growin' up in southeastern Pennsylvania
around lots of fruit trees, she makes a mean crisp.

The Filling
1 tablespoon unsalted butter,
    softened
1 cup sugar
3 tablespoons flour
¼ teaspoon kosher salt
4 large tart apples, peeled,
    cored, and sliced
1 cup whole cranberries, fresh
    or frozen
½ cup raisins
Freshly grated zest of 1 orange

The Topping
6 tablespoons unsalted butter, chilled
¾ cup brown sugar, packed
⅔ cup flour
¼ cup rolled oats, regular or quick
¼ cup chopped walnuts
½ teaspoon kosher salt
¼ teaspoon ground nutmeg
1 teaspoon ground cinnamon

The Accoutrement
Vanilla ice cream

Preheat the oven to 375°. Smear an 8 by 10 by 2-inch baking pan (2 ½-quart capacity) with butter.

Mix up the sugar, flour, and salt in a large bowl. Toss in the apples, cranberries, raisins, and zest. Stir til everything is well mixed, and dump it all into the buttered pan.

Make the topping. Cut the butter into ½-inch cubes and put them in a bowl along with all the remaining ingredients for the topping. Pinch the mixture with your fingers til all the ingredients are evenly coated and crumbly. Sprinkle the topping over the fruit.

Pop the pan into the oven and bake for 45 to 55 minutes, or til the fruit juices are bubbling and the topping is browned. Pull the crisp out of the oven and let it cool for 20 to 30 minutes. Serve warm with a scoop of ice cream. FEEDS 4 TO 6

Note: Cranberries are usually only available around the holidays, so buy a couple of extra bags and freeze them. That way you can make this crisp whenever the mood strikes.

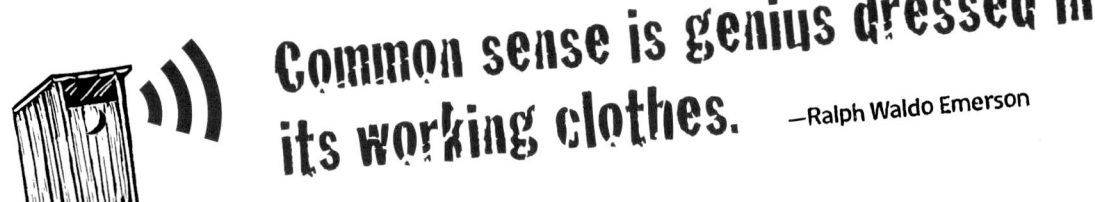

Common sense is genius dressed in its working clothes. —Ralph Waldo Emerson

Dinosaur Pantry

Barbecue Staples

Here's what you're gonna need to make some serious barbecue. We're startin' you out with all the ingredients we use most—chiles, herbs, and spices. You'll find that our cooking won't set your tongue on fire, but it'll stimulate your taste buds with deeply spiced flavors.

Chiles (dried)

Every chile has its own flavor profile. Some are real fruity beneath the heat, some are earthy. Others add smoky notes to your cooking. Chiles are sold either whole or already ground, which makes them easy to use. However, don't confuse pure ground dried chiles with commercial chili powder, which is a blend of several other ingredients. If you can only get the whole chiles, toast them in a dry cast-iron skillet over medium heat before grinding. This will crisp them so they're easier to grind. Just a couple of minutes will do. When they release their aroma, pull them out of the pan and grind them in a mortar with a pestle or in a coffee or spice mill. Make sure you clean up your grinders well afterward. Here are the chiles we use the most at the Dinosaur:

Ancho This is a dried poblano pepper. It should be brick red to dark mahogany, wide at the top and pointy at the bottom. Anchos will add heat along with subtle plum and raisin flavors to your dishes.

Chipotle This is a smoked jalapeño pepper. It has a wrinkled appearance and is brown in color. Smoking concentrates its heat and makes it much hotter than a fresh jalapeño. Along with the smoky flavors, you'll pick up notes of leather, coffee, and wild mushrooms.

Pasilla This chile often gets mixed up with the ancho because it's roughly the same size. However, the pasilla is dark purple-black and wrinkled. Its intensely smoky taste resonates with deep flavors that can range from currants to coffee.

Chiles (fresh)

We're pretty basic in our fresh chile usage. They're chopped up and cooked with the usual onion and pepper flavor base used in so many of our recipes. Look for chiles with bright, smooth, unbroken skin. Store them in the fridge wrapped in paper towels. This keeps them fresher than plastic bags. Protect your hands with latex gloves when cutting chiles and removing seeds and veins. That way the volatile pepper oils that would have you hopping up and down if you were to touch your eyes or mouth get tossed out with the gloves when you're done. Once again, there are many fresh hot peppers, but these are our favorites:

Jalapeño This is a medium to dark green (sometimes red) pepper shaped like a bullet 2 to 3 inches long. It lends heat but not pain to recipes.

Habanero This bad boy looks like a green, yellow, or orange lantern-shaped pepper and is wickedly hot. If you can get past the heat you can detect lots of fruity flavor notes. Use with extreme caution.

Herbs

We like to use fresh herbs whenever possible. However, we do use both fresh and dried herbs in our recipes. If you have to use dried, remember that you use half as much dried as fresh. These are the most commonly used herbs in our recipes:

- Basil
- Bay leaves
- Celery seeds
- Chives
- Cilantro
- Dill
- Oregano
- Parsley, Italian
- Rosemary
- Thyme

Kosher salt

We like Diamond Crystal brand the best. Because the choice of salt makes such a difference in our cooking, be sure to read the following Salt Advisory.

Spices

No barbecue pantry should be without:

- Allspice, ground
- Cayenne pepper
- Chili powder (commercial)
- Cinnamon, ground
- Coriander, ground
- Pepper, black coarse and fine grind
- Peppercorns, black
- Pepper, crushed red
- Cumin, ground
- Five-spice powder
- Lemon pepper
- Mustard seeds
- Nutmeg, ground
- Paprika, Hungarian

Important Salt Advisory

Not all salt is created equal. Granular salt has crystals shaped like dense cubes, the result of its vacuum pan evaporation processing, while kosher salt, the product of surface evaporation, has crystals shaped like flaky pyramids. Think of it as the difference between a snowflake and an ice cube. The snowflake-like crystals of kosher salt stick better to foods, making them essential in rubs. They also melt better and faster into any saucy dish.

That's why we use kosher salt in all of our recipes. But here's the rub. Teaspoon per teaspoon you use more kosher salt than granular salt to season a dish properly. That's why some of our salt quantities look so large, especially because most other people's recipes are written to use granular salt, and that's what you're probably used to.

We used Diamond Kosher Salt when we tested the recipes in this book. So if you find yourself hankering after one of our recipes, but you haven't gotten yourself a box of kosher salt, then be sure to cut our kosher salt quantity in half before substituting granular salt.

Pantry Staples

Because we know that barbecue does not live by smoke alone, here are a few other ingredients you'll need to keep on hand so you can make all these great recipes without a trip to the supermarket.

Basics

Brown sugar We use this to help balance sauces. Look for brown sugar made from pure sugar cane. You can use either dark or light brown sugar. Dark brown sugar has a more intense molasses taste.

Butter Nothing tastes like butter. Fold it into a sauce at the end for a wicked finish. We prefer using unsalted butter, which is usually fresher than salted butter and allows us to control the seasoning.

Buttermilk If you're a corn bread lover, you'll need to keep some buttermilk on hand. It's also great for marinating meats and for dipping fish or chicken fillets in before coating them in crumbs.

Stock or broth We encourage you to make your own and freeze it (pages 168 and 169) for maximum flavor potential. It's a lot of work, but once you taste your own homemade stock, you'll be hooked. In case you run out of the homemade stuff, you might want to have some cans of beef and chicken broth on hand.

Tomatoes (canned) These are always good to have around. Keep a couple of cans of crushed tomatoes and diced tomatoes in both 16-ounce and 28-ounce sizes as well as tomato sauce in 16-ounce cans in your pantry at all times. I like the ones from California, but if you really want to showboat the tomatoes, use the San Marzano brand from Italy.

Wine and spirits Red wine and dry white wine as well as dry marsala are good to keep in your pantry. A splash of bourbon, brandy, or sherry can transform a sauce. They're good to have around, too.

Condiments

These are the "must haves" of the barbecue pantry.

Honey This is a great balancing agent. If your sauce tastes a bit tart, a couple of teaspoons of honey stirred in at the end never fail to do the trick.

Horseradish Grated and preserved in vinegar, horseradish adds a special sinus-clearin' kick to sauces for seafood as well as beef.

Molasses Just like honey, molasses can round out a sauce and give it some mystery along with the sweetness.

Mustard There are many varieties of mustard, and we keep several kinds on hand at all times. We always have a coarse-grain Creole mustard like Zatarain's from Louisiana (see Resources, page 175), a smooth and tart Dijon from France, and a traditional spicy brown mustard from the American heartland.

Soy sauce This ancient Asian flavoring agent is made from fermented soybeans mixed with roasted grain and fortified with yeast. Its salty, distinctive edginess gives an Asian flavor profile to BBQ sauce.

Tabasco sauce This very hot pepper sauce is made only by the McIlhenny Company on Avery Island in the Louisiana Bayou. Splash it in at the end to boost the heat in your dish.

Vinegar We like to use vinegar to add tanginess to dressings and sauces. It's also an indispensable pickling agent. The ones we keep on hand include balsamic, cider, red wine, rice wine, and white vinegar.

Worcestershire sauce Originally from India, this condiment was first made commercially in Worcester, England, by the Lea & Perrins Company. The thin, dark, pungent sauce is a brew of anchovies, chile peppers, cloves, corn syrup, molasses, salt, onions, shallots, tamarind, vinegar, and water. We use it to boost the flavor of sauces, stews, and other dishes.

Cheeses

We don't use a lot of cheese at the Dinosaur, but when we do, we go for the good stuff. Treat your cheese right. Buy hard cheese in wedges and grate your own for best flavor. Keep cheese tightly wrapped in plastic wrap and store in the warmest part of your refrigerator. Change the plastic wrap every time you use the cheese. Here are our favorites:

Cheddar The flavor of most commercial Cheddars has become very bland. For a cheese that will stand up to the bright flavors of barbecue, look for an aged Cheddar. We believe in buying local, so we turn to the Heluva Good Cheese Company, located in Sodus, New York (see Resources, page 174).

Italian grating cheese You don't usually think of these cheeses when you think of barbecue, but I love 'em. It must be the Italian side of me. Use the real thing, and don't cheap out—it's definitely worth it.

> • **Pecorino Romano** is the traditional grating cheese of southern Italy. Look for white wheels with the words "Pecorino Romano" pressed into the rind in dashes and with the sheep's head certification mark surrounded by a diamond.
> • **Parmigiano-Reggiano** is the traditional grating cheese of northern Italy, but it's also a great table cheese. Look for the words "Parmigiano-Reggiano" in pin dots impressed into the rind of the cheese.

Oils

We have come to prefer monounsaturated oils to polyunsaturated oils. Here's what we like to use and when:

Olive oil This is the oil we use most, because it's my favorite. Use olive oil labeled pure for cooking and extra virgin for salads. And remember, not all extra virgins are honest virgins, so be sure to look for the words "cold-pressed" on the label.

Peanut oil Whenever there are Asian flavors being worked into a sauce, our choice is peanut oil. We also like to deep-fry in peanut oil because it has the highest smoking point of any oil.

Sesame oil You need to keep only a small bottle of this pungent oil on hand. We stir it into dishes a teaspoon at a time. You can find it in Asian groceries or in the Asian food section of many supermarkets.

Rice

Long-grain rice (like Carolina) This is a critical ingredient in making a side dish to go along with a lot of our saucy barbecue recipes.

Parboiled long-grain rice (like Uncle Ben's Converted) This is what we use for dishes where the rice gets cooked in with a lot of other ingredients, as in gumbo, jambalaya, and rice pudding.

Mojito Marinade

For years I carted cases of this citrus-flavored Cuban marinade back from Miami, til we started making it in the restaurant. The real thing is all tarted up with the juice of bitter oranges—nearly impossible to find. So we add a touch of lime juice to freshly squeezed orange juice to give it the right kick. It's one of the most versatile pantry ingredients you can make. Use it as a marinade for pork and chicken, pour it over cooked veggies or potatoes, or toss it with salad greens.

¼ cup chopped garlic
½ cup chopped onion
2 cups fresh orange juice
½ cup fresh lime juice
½ cup olive oil

4 teaspoons kosher salt
1 tablespoon black pepper
2 teaspoons ground cumin
2 teaspoons dried oregano
1 tablespoon chopped fresh cilantro

Mix together the garlic, onions, orange juice, and lime juice in a bowl. Heat the olive oil in a large saucepan til just smoking. Now cover up your arms and put some potholder mitts on your hands because you're about to do something that is contrary to good cooking practice but produces great flavor release. Slide the contents of the bowl into the hot oil—be very careful because the liquid will splatter. Simmer for 5 minutes to soften the onions and garlic. Season the marinade with the rest of the ingredients. Pour everything into a blender or food processor and pulse 3 times to combine. Pour into a plastic container and cool to room temperature; then cover and refrigerate. Mojito Marinade keeps for up to 2 weeks. MAKES 2 ½ CUPS

Mop Sauce

To mop or not to mop, that is the question. There seem to be two schools of thought about moppin' ribs while they're cookin'. Personally, I think that if the ribs look dry and thirsty you should mop 'em. Mop sauce should never contain sugars that would burn before the ribs are cooked through. A good mop sauce is based on the spicy flavors of the rub.

1 cup white vinegar
½ cup water
2 tablespoons vegetable oil
2 tablespoons Worcestershire sauce

2 tablespoons All-Purpose Red Rub
(page 167)
Tabasco sauce

Throw everything together in a saucepan and bring to a boil. Cool, pour into a plastic container, cover, and refrigerate for later use. MAKES 1 ¾ CUPS

Mutha Sauce

Just like the name says, this is the basis—the true mother of all the sauces we have in this book. It is a balanced blend of sweet, savory, spicy, and smoky flavors that acts as our leapin' off point for creating a world of barbecue sensations. It can even stand alone as a traditional slatherin' sauce for ribs and chicken. Now being the shameless promoter that I am, I gotta inform you that there's a fine line of Dinosaur barbecue sauces. So if you don't feel like jerkin' around cookin' the Mutha Sauce, just check out Dinosaur Bar-B-Que Sensuous Slathering Sauce (page 174).

¼ cup vegetable oil

1 cup minced onion

½ cup minced green pepper

1 jalapeño pepper, seeded and minced

Pinch each of kosher salt and black pepper

2 tablespoons minced garlic

1 can (28 ounces) tomato sauce

2 cups ketchup (preferably Heinz)

1 cup water

¾ cup Worcestershire sauce

½ cup cider vinegar

¼ cup lemon juice

¼ cup molasses

¼ cup cayenne pepper sauce

¼ cup spicy brown mustard

¾ cup dark brown sugar, packed

1 tablespoon chili powder

2 teaspoons coarsely ground black pepper

½ teaspoon ground allspice

1 tablespoon Liquid Smoke (optional)

Pour the oil into a large saucepan and set over medium-high heat. Toss in the onions, green peppers, and jalapeños and give them a stir. Season with a pinch of salt and pepper and cook til soft and golden. Add the garlic and cook for 1 minute more. Dump in everything else except the Liquid Smoke. Bring to a boil, then lower the heat so the sauce simmers. Simmer for 10 minutes. Swirl in the Liquid Smoke and let the sauce cool. Pour it into a container, cover, and store in the fridge til ready to use.
MAKES 6 TO 7 CUPS

Variation: Hot BBQ Sauce

Add 2 or 3 seeded and minced habanero peppers (about 1 ½ teaspoons to 1 tablespoon) along with the onions, peppers, and jalapeños. Also add ½ teaspoon cayenne pepper along with the other ingredients for extra punch.

Danger!!!
Working with habaneros can cause plenty of personal pain and suffering if you're not careful. Never touch the cut flesh or seeds with your bare hands. While it won't sting your hands (unless you've got a cut), the volatile oils from the peppers get into your pores and can be transferred to your eyes or other moist, sensitive areas on your body long after you're done cookin'. Even washing your hands doesn't help. So wear latex gloves while working with habaneros and be sure to protect your hands while cleaning up your cutting board and knife as well. Then toss out the gloves.

All-Purpose Red Rub

Rubbin' spices into meat is the essential first step of great barbecue. This is a good starter rub, but feel free to personalize it. Add some of your favorite herbs or pulverized dried smoked chiles. Just make sure you keep the sweet, savory, and spicy flavors in balance.

½ cup paprika

½ cup kosher salt

½ cup light brown sugar

½ cup granulated garlic

6 tablespoons granulated onion

¼ cup chili powder

1 tablespoon black pepper

1 teaspoon ground cumin

½ teaspoon cayenne pepper

 **Dump** all the ingredients into a bowl and rub them together with your hands.

Store in a plastic or glass container til ready to use.
MAKES 2 ¾ CUPS

Creole Seasoning

This is the lusty cousin of our All-Purpose Red Rub (see above). It'll make whatever you rub it into earthy, spicy, and complex. But don't use it only on meat destined for barbecue; sprinkle it on anything you're grillin', including veggies. Mix it into bread crumbs before coating food, or stir it into a casserole. It's a great flavor-boostin' agent.

½ cup paprika

½ cup granulated garlic

¼ cup granulated onion

3 tablespoons black pepper

2 teaspoons white pepper

2 teaspoons cayenne pepper

¼ cup dried oregano

¼ cup dried thyme

2 teaspoons ground cumin

2 tablespoons sugar

 **Combine** everything in a bowl and mix it up real well. Store in a plastic or glass container with a lid.   MAKES 2 ½ CUPS

Chicken Stock

Homemade stock is the foundation of all truly great soups and stews.
Not everyone has the time to make it, but if you do you'll find it really
makes a difference in your cooking.

4 to 5 pounds chicken backs, necks,
    legs, and thighs
Kosher salt and black pepper
1 large onion, unpeeled, cut into 8 chunks
3 stalks celery, washed and cut in large pieces
3 large carrots, peeled and cut in large pieces

4 large cloves garlic, peeled and crushed
Small handful of fresh Italian parsley
2 bay leaves
1 tablespoon dried thyme
2 cups plus 3 quarts water

Preheat the oven to 375°. Pull any obvious hunks of fat off the chicken pieces, and place the chicken in a single layer in a roasting pan. Season the pieces generously with salt and pepper. When the oven is hot, pop the chicken in and roast for 45 minutes. While that's going on, put the onion, celery, carrots, garlic, parsley, bay leaves, and thyme in a soup pot.

Pull the chicken out of the oven when it's done, and put the pieces in the soup pot. Skim off the fat from the roasting pan and pour in 2 cups of water. Set the pan over medium heat on top of the stove and stir, scraping in all the tasty browned meat juices clinging to the sides and bottom of the pan. Pour these pan juices into the soup pot, along with 3 more quarts of water.

Set the pot over high heat and bring quickly to a boil. As soon as it starts to bubble, knock the heat down to low and simmer the stock. As the ingredients in the pot heat, a scum will rise to the surface. Skim it off every 5 minutes or so til it

stops appearing. Cook, uncovered, about 3 hours to pull the flavor out of the ingredients and into the stock.

Skim as much fat off the top as you can. Then line a large colander with several layers of dampened cheesecloth. Set the colander over another large pot and strain the stock. Press down on the veggies and meat with the bottom of a small bowl to squeeze out any remaining liquid.

Season the stock to taste with kosher salt. Pour the stock into quart containers and chill, uncovered, in the fridge, til the fat solidifies on the surface. Remove the fat and discard. Cover the stock and use within several days, or label and freeze for use later.   MAKES ABOUT 2 TO 2 ½ QUARTS

Note: You can also freeze stock in ice cube trays til hard; then pop the cubes out and store them in a plastic resealable bag. Now they're ready for you to toss into pan sauces to rev up the flavor. Each cube is about 1 tablespoon of stock.

Beef Stock

Makin' your own stock is a bit time-consuming, but the reward is in the depth of flavor it brings to any dish. There's nothing hard about the preparation, and it makes your house smell delicious.

5 pounds meaty beef soup bones
   (such as shanks or ribs)
2 medium onions, quartered
2 carrots, peeled and cut in large chunks
¼ cup vegetable oil
Kosher salt and black pepper

2 cups plus 4 quarts water
3 stalks celery, cut in large chunks
6 large cloves garlic, peeled and crushed
2 bay leaves
Small handful of fresh Italian parsley
1 tablespoon tomato paste

Preheat the oven to 450°. Arrange the beef bones, onions, and carrots in a large roasting pan. Drizzle with oil and season with salt and pepper. Pop the pan into the oven and roast for 90 minutes, turning the pieces every 15 minutes til the meat is deeply browned.

Scoop
the meat and veggies out of the roasting pan and put them in a large soup pot. Skim off the fat in the roasting pan. Set the pan over medium heat on top of the stove and add 2 cups of water. Heat, stirring constantly and scraping up all the brown juices clinging to the sides and bottom of the pan. Pour the liquid into the soup pot.

Add the celery, garlic, bay leaves, parsley, and tomato paste to the pot. Cover the ingredients with 4 quarts of water and set the pot over high heat. Bring it quickly to a boil. As soon as it starts to bubble, knock the heat down to low and simmer the stock. As the ingredients in the pot heat, a scum will rise to the surface. Skim it off every 5 minutes or so til it stops appearing.

Simmer
gently, uncovered, for 4 hours to pull every bit of flavor out of the meat. Line a large colander with several layers of dampened cheesecloth. Set the colander over another large pot and strain the stock. Season to taste with salt. Pour into quart containers and chill, uncovered, in the fridge. Once chilled, lift off and discard the fat that has come to the surface. Cover the stock and use it in a couple of days, or label and freeze for use later. MAKES 8 TO 12 CUPS

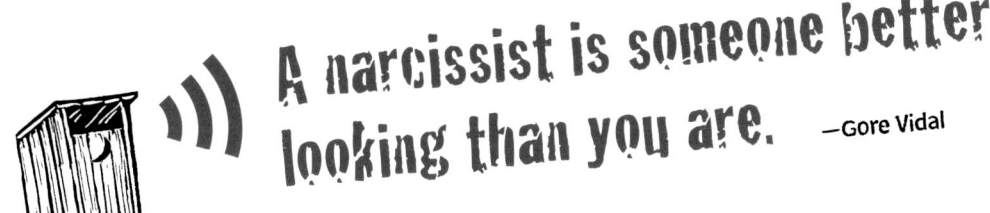

A narcissist is someone better looking than you are. —Gore Vidal

Roasted Garlic

This classic ingredient comes in handy. Double or triple the recipe and keep some in the fridge at all times for seasonin' bread, sauce, or your best friend.

2 large bulbs garlic
Olive oil

Kosher salt and black pepper

Preheat the oven to 375°. Cut the top off of each bulb, slicing into the points of the cloves. Place them cut side up on a piece of foil. Drizzle with oil and sprinkle with salt and pepper. Wrap the foil up around the bulbs and bake for 45 to 60 minutes, til they release their perfume. Open the foil and test for doneness. The cloves should squeeze softly when pinched. Bake a little longer if they seem to need it. Roasted garlic keeps for several days in the fridge. MAKES 2 BULBS

Blue Cheese Dressing

This is a thick dressing perfect for dippin' hot-from-the-grill Chicken Wings (page 19) in. If you want to serve it as a salad dressing, thin it down by adding a bit of milk slowly at the end.

2 cups mayonnaise
3 tablespoons apple cider vinegar
1 teaspoon Worcestershire sauce
2 tablespoons lemon juice
1 teaspoon dry mustard

½ teaspoon white pepper
¼ teaspoon celery seed
Tabasco sauce
¾ cup crumbled blue cheese

Whisk together everything but the Tabasco and blue cheese in a storage bowl with a lid. Spice it up with the Tabasco, then gently stir in the cheese, preserving the nice chunky texture. Cover and refrigerate til ready to use. Keeps for 2 weeks. MAKES 2 CUPS

Cayenne Buttermilk Ranch Dressing

We use this versatile dressing on more than just salad greens. It makes a good dip-pin' sauce for fried or grilled meats and veggies as well as a sauce for Chicken-Fried Chicken sandwiches (page 69) and Fried Green Tomatoes (page 28).

1 ¼ cups mayonnaise

1 cup buttermilk

1 tablespoon red wine vinegar

2 teaspoons minced garlic

¼ cup finely chopped chives

1 tablespoon lemon pepper

¼ cup freshly grated
     Parmigiano-Reggiano cheese

1 teaspoon kosher salt

Freshly ground black pepper

1 teaspoon Creole Seasoning (page 167)

Whisk all the ingredients together in a bowl. Pour into a container with a lid, and store in the fridge til needed.
MAKES 2 ½ CUPS

Dough for One-Crust Pie

1 ½ cups flour
½ teaspoon kosher salt
¼ cup butter, chilled

¼ cup lard, chilled
3 to 4 tablespoons ice water

Toss the flour and salt into the workbowl of a food processor and pulse a couple of times to combine. Cut the butter into ¼-inch cubes and sprinkle them over the flour in the workbowl. Add the lard in 2 or 3 pieces. Process with 15 rapid on-off pulses or just til the biggest lumps of flour-covered fat are no bigger than a few small peas. Add 3 tablespoons of ice water through the feed tube and pulse 5 times. Feel the dough and make sure it's just damp enough to hold together when you squeeze a bit in your hand. If not, add the last tablespoon of water and pulse 5 more times. The dough will be loose and ragged (don't overprocess it into a ball).

Dump the dough out onto a work surface. Push the dough with the heel of your hand 2 or 3 times to flatten out some of the lumps of fat. Then gather the dough into a ball. Flour the work surface and roll the dough out with a floured rolling pin into a circle 12 ½ inches in diameter. Fold the dough in half and put it into a 9-inch pie pan. Unfold it and press it into the pan, trimming the edges if you need to. Roll the edge under and shape a high fluted edge all around. Toss the finished pie shell into the freezer to chill while making the filling.   MAKES 1 PIE CRUST FOR A 9-INCH PIE PAN

Resources

RESOURCES

Dinosaur Bar-B-Que Restaurants

Syracuse
246 West Willow Street
Syracuse, NY 13202
315-476-4937
Hours: Monday to Thursday, 11 a.m. to 2 a.m. (kitchen open til 12 midnight) Friday and Saturday, 11 a.m. to 2 a.m. (kitchen open til 1 a.m.) Sunday, 4 p.m. to 9 p.m.

Rochester
99 Court Street
Rochester, NY 14604
716-325-7090
Hours: Monday to Thursday, 11 a.m. to 2 a.m. (kitchen open til 12 midnight) Friday and Saturday, 11 a.m. to 2 a.m. (kitchen open to 1 a.m.) Sunday, closed

(all major credit cards accepted)

Dinosaur Bar-B-Que Products

246 West Willow Street
Syracuse, NY 13202
315-476-1662
888-476-1662 (toll free)
Fax: 315-476-1663
E-mail: info@dinobbq.com
Web site: www.dinobbq.com

- **Dinosaur Bar-B-Que Sensuous Slathering Sauce**
  A good substitute for the Mutha Sauce (page 165)
- **Dinosaur Bar-B-Que Roasted Garlic & Honey Bar-B-Que Sauce**
- **Dinosaur Bar-B-Que Wango Tango Hot Habanero Bar-B-Que Sauce**
  A good substitute for Hot BBQ Sauce (page 165)
- **Devil's Duel Hot Habanero Pepper Sauce**
- **A.H.U. (All Hopped Up) Garlic Chipotle Hot Pepper Sauce**
- **Cajun Foreplay Spice Rub**
  A good substitute for Creole Seasoning (page 167)

- **Mojito Marinade and Dressing**
  A good substitute for Mojito Marinade (page 164)

Note: Each of the above brand names are the registered trademarks or the common law trademarks of Dino-store, Inc.

Ingredients

Cheeses

Heluva Good Cheese, Inc.
P.O. Box 410
6551 Pratt Road
Sodus, NY 14551
315-483-6971
800-323-2188 (toll free)
Fax: 315-483-9927
Web site: www.heluvagood.com

- Naturally aged cheeses, real sour cream dips, and condiments

Chiles, BBQ Sauces, Hot Sauces

The Hot Shoppe
311 South Clinton Street
Syracuse, NY 13202
315-424-1010
888-HOT-EATS (toll free)
Fax: 315-424-0165
E-mail: hotshoppe@hotshoppe.com
Web site: www.hotshoppe.com

Wharton Pepper Co.
Route 3, Box 124-L
Monticello, FL 32344
850-997-4359
Fax: 850-997-1429
E-mail: wharton@sauceboss.com
Website: www.sauceboss.com

- **Bill Wharton's Liquid Summer Datil Pepper Hot Sauce**
- **Liquid Summer Habanero Hot Sauce**

Note: Each of the above brand names are the registered trademarks or the common law trademarks of the Wharton Pepper Co.

Creole Mustard

Zatarain's
82 First Street
P.O. Box 347
Gretna, LA 70053
504-367-2950
Fax 504-362-2004
Web site: www.zatarain.com

Fish and Seafood

Fins and Tails Seafood Store
3012 Erie Boulevard East
Syracuse, NY 13224
315-446-5417
Website: www.finsandtails.com

Italian Ingredients

Lombardi's Imports (two locations)
534 Butternut Street
Syracuse, NY 13208
315-472-5900
Fax: 315-472-2206
website: www.LombardisImports.com

124 North Main Street
Fairport, NY 14450
716-388-1330
Fax: 716-388-9275
Web site: www.LombardisGourmet.com

• Cheese, salami, and imported Italian specialties

Sausages

Gianelli Sausage Co.
P.O. Box 10
111 Luther Avenue
Liverpool, NY 13088
315-471-9164
Fax: 315-471-4474
E-mail: gianelli@twcny.rr.com
Web site: www.gianellisausage.com

• Hot or sweet Italian pork sausage, chorizo, andouille, and kielbasa

Turkey

Plainville Farms
7830 Plainville Road
Plainville, NY 13137
315-638-0226
800-724-0206 (toll free)
Fax: 315-638-0659
E-mail: bquijano@plainvillefarms.com
Web site: www.plainvillefarms.com

• Fresh turkey raised without the routine use of antibiotics and without animal by-products: fresh whole turkey, turkey breast, turkey tenderloins, ground turkey, boneless turkey roast, and smoked whole turkey and turkey breast

Pits, Smokers, and Grills

BBQ Pits by Klose
2216 West 34th Street
Houston, TX 77018
800-487-7487 (toll free)
Fax: 713-686-8793
E-mail: bbqpits@msn.com
Web site: www.bbqpits.com

Smoking Woods and Charwood

Peoples Woods/Nature's Own
75 Mill Street
Cumberland, RI 02864
800-729-5800 (toll free)
Fax: 401-725-0006
Web site: www.peopleswoods.com

• Wood chips and chunks made from 100 percent natural hardwoods in alder, apple, ash, beechwood, birch, cherry, grapevine, hickory, maple, mesquite, oak, peach, and sassafras

Artists

Elliott Mattice
689 Allen Street
Syracuse, NY 13210
315-475-9346
E-mail: geocities.com/elliottmattice
Web site: www.nycentral.com/mattice

- Retro/pop imagery from the '50s and '60s—painting, posters, graphic design, and murals

Jeff Davies
460 Westcott Street
Syracuse, NY 13210
315-474-0150
E-mail: kunst999@aol.com

- Work shown on end papers and table of contents

- Murals, paintings, sculpture, commissions, demolitions, and small wars

Commander Cody
P.O. Box 900
Saratoga, NY 12866
Web site: www.commandercody.com

- Work shown on page 128

- Portraits of blues greats in oil or marker

Tattoo Artists

Al Cramer
Central NY Tattoo Co.
51 Goodfellow Road
Fulton, NY 13069
315-638-8288
Hours: By appointment
E-mail: flyink@aol.com

Index

C